THE RACK we BUILT

THE RACK we BUILT

THE GOOD THE BAD AND THE UGLY OF CREATING COMPANY CULTURE

LORENZO GOMEZ III

geekdom media

THE RACK WE BUILT

The Good, The Bad, and the Ugly of Creating Company Culture

ISBN   978-1-5445-1425-3 *Hardcover*

      978-1-5445-1424-6 *Paperback*

      978-1-5445-1423-9 *Ebook*

This book is dedicated to all Rackers—past, present, and future.

Once a Racker, always a Racker.

Contents

Introduction

I've had the good fortune to work with serial entrepreneur and philanthropist Graham Weston since 2001. During that time, I've increased my knowledge about business and life a thousand-fold, but there's one phrase in particular that changed my life forward from the day I heard Graham say it. That phrase is the foundation of this book and is one any company that wants to create a thriving people-centric culture can live by:

Everyone wants to be a valued member of a winning team on an inspiring mission.

Take a minute and let that sink in. Think about the places you've worked, the companies you've founded. It's true, isn't it? It's so obvious you might even be asking yourself, "Why didn't I think of that?"

To set the record straight, Graham wasn't the first person to come up with the idea or say that phrase, but he saw the power of it and passed it on to me.

I once asked Graham where the phrase came from. He told me, "Lorenzo, in life, we don't always get to come up with the big ideas, but you should always strive to be the person who never lets an amazing idea pass you by. I didn't come up with the idea for Rackspace, but the moment I saw it I knew what a powerful idea it was, and I seized it." He explained that a couple of years after Rackspace went public, he'd been on a call with Fred Reichheld, the founder of Net Promoter Score (NPS), which tracks customer loyalty metrics for big companies. NPS evaluates customer satisfaction by asking one and a half questions: "Would you refer my service or my company to a friend or colleague, and why?" Their conversation focused on how big companies can actually use NPS internally to evaluate each department like it is its own business. You can quickly see what department is the least helpful when all the other departments give them a low NPS. During their conversation, Fred said, "Everyone wants to be a valued member of a winning team on an inspiring mission." And Graham wrote it down as the conversation continued.

Later that day, Graham called Fred to tell him the phrase was a game-changing idea, and he planned to make it the cornerstone of the Rackspace culture.

It is befitting that Fred Reichheld, the man who dedicated his life to the study of customer loyalty and what good companies do to earn that loyalty, also instinctively realized what it takes for employees to pledge their undying loyalty to a company.

While the success of the organization itself creates the winning team, an inspiring mission drives an organization's culture, and core values guide the actions that make employees feel like valued members. This isn't a twenty-first century idea—this has been going on as long as organizations have had employees. Let me give you a couple of examples.

Ernest Shackleton is one of the most famous British explorers. His story of sailing to the South Pole is epic. He put an ad in a London newspaper that said:

Men wanted for hazardous journey, small wages, bitter cold, long months of complete darkness, constant danger. Safe return doubtful. Honor and recognition in case of success.

Legend has it, Shackleton received more than five thousand responses. It wasn't just about people wanting adventure; he intuitively tapped into men's desire to be *valued members* of a *winning team* on an *inspiring mission.*

Walt Disney changed the world of movies by adding sound

and color to silent, black-and-white motion pictures—something Disney's critics told him couldn't be done. After Snow White sang and danced across the screen followed by her colorful band of dwarves, Disney went on a recruiting spree. The top animators at the time jumped at the chance to leave Popeye and Bugs Bunny behind to bring Mickey, Pinocchio, and Bambi to life, even when it meant taking a pay cut. If you were an animator in 1938, you couldn't help but want to be part of Disney's creations. Neal Gabler writes in *Walt Disney: The Triumph of the American Imagination,*[1] "One animator, obviously proud of the new Disney cachet as the best animation studio, said that working there made them all feel 'as if we were members of the same class at West Point.'" This was a generation that went to work for one reason: to provide for their families. This was a time when duty was the main reason to get out of bed and go to work. Then, one day, Walt Disney showed up and led his company based on something so uncommon for that day and age.

Walt Disney led them with an *inspiring mission.*

Way before there were open floor plans and free soda machines, Walt Disney took a bunch of eccentric animators who were previously seen as beasts-of-burden cartoonists and made them feel like the *valued members,* which they

---

1   Neal Gabler, *Walt Disney: The Triumph of the American Imagination*, Alfred A. Knopf, 2006 (New York).

were, of the whole process. And the entertainment industry hasn't been the same since.

A WINNING TEAM ON AN INSPIRING MISSION: RACKSPACE

When I went to work at Rackspace in 2001, I felt like Shackleton's sailors or Disney's animators must have felt. Rackspace was in the managed hosting business—possibly the least sexy piece of the tech world that's basically the plumbing of the internet. I would soon discover that its mission was so inspiring that I would dedicate the next decade of my life to it. How could I be anything but excited to work for the company that helped introduce YouTube to the world and fundamentally changed the internet?

From the very beginning, the Rackspace leadership somehow knew that they had to form a *winning team* to compete in the managed hosting space. The original three founders, Richard Yoo, Dirk Elmendorf, and Patrick Condon, formed their founding team out of their Trinity University dorm room in San Antonio. Knowing they needed additional investment and business know-how, they pitched San Antonio business legends Graham Weston and Morris Miller, who both invested and joined the leadership team. Lastly, they recruited Lanham Napier and Lew Moorman. Napier and Moorman became the critical executives who helped carry the company to its eventual IPO in 2008.

I'd never met innovative, visionary businesspeople like the Rackspace leaders, and I knew they were special. I was intimidated by every single one of them because they were so smart, and I felt more insecure than I had in my entire life. I was a twenty-year-old young man, and I looked up to these guys so much—and still do. I didn't know much, but I did know this one thing: They were a winning team, and if I watched and learned from them, I could be a winner too.

In 2001 the managed hosting competition was ferocious. Most of the companies we competed against were focused on speed, price, and having the latest and greatest hardware. They also had tons of capital. Rackspace, on the other hand, made customer support our priority. Nothing about Rackspace made sense at the time. In a day and age when all the tech companies were in Silicon Valley, people laughed at us for being a tech company based in San Antonio, Texas. Operating in San Antonio, however, with lower rents and salaries than Silicon Valley, allowed us to focus more on the customer with less capital.

While most tech companies hid from their customers, Rackspace gave ours *fanatical support*. Tech, by nature, is a behind-the-scenes business, but what we did was even more behind-the-scenes. Don't believe me? Next time you go into a bar, tell them you do managed hosting for a living and see how many phone numbers you get. Add it all up, and Rackspace should have failed out of the gate by the business and technology world's standards. So why did it succeed?

The Rackspace leadership team knew that the world needed us to do something that no one else could do. They inspired an army of "Rackers" to follow their lead and change our piece of the internet universe. But how?

I didn't have the words to describe it at the time. In fact, it wasn't until almost the end of my Rackspace career that I heard Graham summed up this feeling in that one sentence. I've come to realize that this sentence represents a philosophy worth an entire book. In the pages that follow, I'll prove just how much insight this one sentence contains.

CULTURE STARTS AT THE TOP

Most entrepreneurs start their businesses because they are passionate about the problem they're solving and believe their product or service meets customers' needs better than any other on the market. Solving that problem and bringing something new into the world becomes their—and the organization's—mission. Their passion for that mission inspires everyone in the company. When a company has two or three people, that passion spreads from the leader to the employees faster than a Baby Yoda meme on the internet. Yet, as a company scales and grows and more people come on board, not everyone has direct contact with the leader. How does a leader make sure everyone feels that passion and knows the mission the company is on?

In a word, culture.

But where does culture come from?

Culture is born out of the mission, which keeps the mundane pieces of the work from becoming miserable drudgery. When I joined Rackspace, the official mission was: "To be recognized as one of the world's greatest service companies." At first, it struck me as odd because I thought I was working for a tech company, but in fact, I was working at a service company that provided technical tools. With one mission statement, the company recalibrated my mindset.

The world is full of seemingly boring, repetitive jobs—dishwasher, cashier, managed hosting account manager. Nobody wakes up and says, "I can't wait to get me some managed hosting," but they will jump up at being part of the new internet world. At Rackspace, replacing a broken hard drive wasn't all that exciting, but being one of the world's greatest service companies of all time? Now that was something to write home about!

When your employees wake up thinking, "Yeah, I'm going to answer phones all day, but I'm part of something bigger than myself, something so grand it's worth my time to give my best today," they go to work inspired. People need a reason not to hit the snooze button in the morning, and it's the mission that makes them want to jump out of bed and run to work.

If you think about successful organizations such as Patagonia, Zappos, SpaceX, Pixar, Southwest Airlines, and Navy Seals that are known for their culture, you find those organizations have an inspiring mission. They also make sure their employees feel like valued members of a winning team.

There are business plans and profit and loss statements. One shows you what you want to do, and one shows you the result of what you do. But what about the middle? Culture is how you get people to execute the middle. Telling your employees, "Do exactly what I tell you," is one way to get the plan executed, and that's one type of distinct culture.

The other way to execute the middle is to point to the top of a mountain that you are all going to climb, tell them the plan, and give them principles and guidance for how to get there. That is a very different type of culture and is what I experienced at Rackspace. That is what this book is about.

LIFE BEFORE RACKSPACE

In the jobs I held before joining Rackspace, I had pieces of the culture puzzle. As a teenager, I followed in my siblings' footsteps and worked at the local supermarket chain, H-E-B. In the grocery world of South Texas, H-E-B is *the* winning team. I loved working there, and looking back, I certainly felt like a valued member of that winning team. I'm sure H-E-B had an awesome mission. Even if I didn't know what it was, I could feel it from my place at the bottom of the totem pole. I knew we were there to serve the neighborhood and make it better, offering the goods customers wanted at the best prices and quality.

I left H-E-B to work for Gateway Computers, my first foray into technology. My friend Dax Moreno lured me to Gateway, and many of my friends worked there. Gateway's official mission was something like "bringing computers to the masses at a reasonable price," but to me, the mission seemed to be "beat Dell," which wasn't inspiring at all. Nonetheless, Dax and my other friends were a winning team. I was hired as a receptionist but was quickly promoted to work in sales. I felt like a valued member—until I didn't.

I'm not ashamed to say, I may be the worst salesperson in the history of Gateway—or any company for that matter. I had no understanding of selling value. If a customer asked me how they could save money on a $1,000 computer, I'd suggest they drop the $150 warranty. No salesperson worth their salt would say that. A good salesperson would say, "Based on what you've told me, Mr. Customer, you're going to need that warranty because you're going to use your computer a lot and the more you use it, the more likely it is to break." Shortly after my promotion to sales, Gateway signed a partnership with OfficeMax, whereby they setup sales kiosks inside the OfficeMax stores. Because I had yet to actually hit my sales quota, I was exiled to a sales kiosk in the nearest OfficeMax.

I spent more time directing customers to aisle 19 for the printer paper than selling Gateway products. I sat in my cubicle-jail in the corner of OfficeMax waiting for customers and was so bored I decided to learn to type. I cheated my way through typing class in high school, so I thought I should actually learn the skill since I was a "computer guy" now. One day I was practicing "The quick brown fox jumps over the lazy dog" on my Gateway computer when my friend James Brehm called. He told me he was working for a crazy company I'd never heard of, Rackspace, and they were looking for account managers for their rapidly growing customer base. He said, "You have a servant's heart, Lorenzo, and you'd thrive here." He convinced me to come in for an interview.

I'm pretty sure I got the job based on his recommendation because I didn't even know what hosting was. James told the hiring manager a story about how we were standing around at OfficeMax on a slow day, all talking around the cash register. There was one family in the store. Someone saw that a kid had just puked in the kids' center. James told Rackspace how, without blinking, I said, "I got it," and immediately went and cleaned it up. Thank God I did because it got me the most transformative job in my life. James essentially said, "My friend lives the Rackspace culture and core values, and I have a story to prove it."

As soon as I began that job, I knew Rackspace was different than any other place I'd worked. I remember working late one Saturday night, and I looked out the window of the seventh floor at downtown San Antonio where our office was. I stood there, a wide-eyed young man from the inner city and thought, *"Wow, I work for a tech company downtown. I'm so Sex and The City."*

H-E-B and Gateway were established companies with a longstanding culture. I was pretty far removed from the leaders and had only a vague sense of the mission. Yes, at H-E-B I felt like a valued member of a winning team, but at Gateway, I watched the winning team from the sidelines. Rackspace was a startup. The company had been in business less than three years when I joined as one of the first one hundred employees. This was an opportunity to participate in building the foundation of the culture. I didn't realize at the time how truly magical the environment and experience would be, nor that I would have the chance to live out what it meant to be a valued member of a winning team on an inspiring mission.

LEAD YOUR VALUED MEMBERS OF A WINNING TEAM ON AN INSPIRING MISSION

A handful of articles and books have been written about Rackspace's culture and *fanatical support*. This book is not a tell-all or exposé about Rackspace history. Here, you'll read my personal stories of the time I spent at Rackspace, from when it was a struggling, young startup to shortly after it went public. During that time, almost every day was a lesson in building and sustaining culture. We lived the good, the bad, and the ugly of corporate culture. I believe we got a lot right at the beginning—planned or not—and made some mistakes as we grew into a full-fledged publicly traded company. But what company doesn't make some mistakes?

If you care about the people who work with you or success in general, you must embrace culture as one of your primary responsibilities. Through my stories, I'll share ideas and insight of how you can build a positive, consistent culture in your organization whether you're just starting up, scaling to the next level, or need to get your culture back on track.

When your employees feel your passion for the mission, they'll be excited about the work they do. Their jobs become less about the tasks themselves and more about the greater good. In chapter one, we'll begin by exploring what you need to know about the cornerstones of any successful culture: core values.

Chapter 1

Core Values are Born, Not Manufactured

In the internet world, there is a form of hacking called a Denial of Service, or DoS, attack. Essentially, a hacker activates millions of zombie computers to throw all their traffic at your server at once and it brings down your whole network—a DoS attack. The result is sort of like what happened when Jennifer Aniston joined Instagram.

Graham Weston, one of the founders of Rackspace, used to joke that in our early days, Rackspace had a Denial of Service model for our customers. We didn't want to serve them. It wasn't that we hated our customers, but this was the industry standard of the day. All the experts and investors said that the way to run a profitable tech company was to avoid adding humans at all costs. Giving customers good service requires you to have lots of humans, and humans were too expensive. The solution was to automate everything. The modern-day version of this is the phone system maze and outsourcing to overseas. The standard response when a customer called customer support was, "I'm sorry, you need to submit this issue online. Then the customer would go online and submit the issue, and they would get an automated email that said, "I'm sorry you need to call in for this." This is a tech company's passive-aggressive way of telling you to go away and fix it yourself. Perhaps no one said it to our faces, but I can imagine Rackspace's reputation was the anti-customer company. Close your eyes and imagine that time you called a big company trying to get help, and they did everything they could to avoid you—that was Rackspace in those early days.

The executives decided they needed a leader who cared about customers. After a wide search, they found that quality in David Bryce. Graham first met David in the fall of 1999 when they both attended a meeting for Open Book Management Practitioners. David owned a cleaning company, and Graham was impressed by David's passion for customers. Graham and Morris then invited David to a Young Entrepreneurs Organization (YEO) meeting and gave him the pitch to join the Rackspace team. After a two-hour meeting and a follow-up breakfast the next morning at Jim's Diner (our execs always held the most important business meetings at places with endless coffee and good pie), David finally agreed to leave the cleaning business and join Rackspace as the VP of customer care and as employee number 13. Upon his arrival, all of the tech guys cheered for joy—not because they were excited about David Bryce but because now they had someone to dump all the angry customers on.

David was brought into Rackspace to lead customer support. He was the complete opposite of a DoS attack; he was the godfather of the idea that would come to be known as "*fanatical support*." David cared about people and customers in particular and introduced the idea of customer-centric behavior to Rackspace. He began to change the culture from his first day.

I interviewed David to learn more about that time. He remembered those early days shortly after he'd joined Rackspace. He said, "Customers were complaining all the time. The phones wouldn't stop ringing because the network sucked, and we always had outages. But it wasn't entirely the team's fault. We had five guys trying to provide 24/7 support. We didn't have any tools and were using a lousy open source customer ticketing system. We also had the wrong attitude toward our customers. At the time we very much thought of the business as a real estate business. We hadn't given much thought to customer support."

During those early days, Rackspace only offered Linux, which is an open-source (free) server operating system. They thought because of this, they would only attract tech-savvy customers, but instead, they attracted bootstrap entrepreneurs. And because the entrepreneurs were not Linux experts, they needed help with their servers. Help that we didn't necessarily want to give them.

"I got beat up a lot that first month," David told me. Then one day, he overheard a technician say, "If he doesn't know how to do that, he shouldn't even have a server."

That was the last straw.

"After that, I locked myself in an office for two or three days and wrote the manifesto with ten rules. I wanted us to be *obsessed* with taking care of customers. I opened my thesaurus and "fanatical" was one word that conveyed that.

It was a moment of epiphany. David hadn't thought about the phrase *fanatical support* before then and ran the idea by Graham before he was to present it to the rest of the team. He said, "Graham was very supportive of the idea. He felt that we had a moral obligation to help our customers when they called."

When David rolled out his *fanatical support* theory to the team, his speech was simple and direct. But since I wasn't there, I chose to believe that it was a more powerful techie version of Al Pacino's speech at the end of *Scent of a Woman*. The team got it right away, and the perspective of the entire company changed. **Fanatical support** made us "Rackers" special. It was a value that mobilized us and gave us purpose. It didn't come forth from a consultant's market research or a marketing focus group. It came from David being fed up with how terribly we were treating our customers, but until he pointed it out, we didn't really believe there was a different, better way. **Fanatical support** was a game-changing idea. And so, the first core value was born.

In our conversation, David said, "The culture is the personality of the organization." Everyone sees your culture: the good moods, the bad moods, the kindness and authenticity, the wisdom, and the outbursts.

I would add that your core values are your immune system. Your core values are less visible but equally important to keeping culture healthy and fighting off foreign bodies or bad influences. Your core values happen on the inside, providing support when culture is wavering and raising the red flags when something is wrong. When your culture is healthy, you're unstoppable.

GET YOUR CORE VALUES RIGHT

Your core values provide a litmus test for every decision you or anyone else makes in your organization. An organization gut check if you will. Your core values should stand the test of time and allow every employee to do three things:

- Hire people
- Fire people
- Make decisions when the leader isn't around

You should also have a story for each one that could be told at the water cooler. These stories are what bring the core values to life and allow the employees to spread the values organically.

Yet, so many organizations get this wrong. They use important-sounding words and create fake, fluffy, glittery "values" that really mean nothing. Things like, "We're passionate about integrity." What does that even mean? It's easy to fall into this trap; we had one of these values at Rackspace, which you'll read about in the next chapter.

We didn't set out to state what kind of company we wanted to build or the core values we wanted to practice. On the contrary, it coincided with a period where we would all agree that it was not performing the way we wanted. The core values were born out of a season of adversity in the beginning.

When I arrived at Rackspace, there were six people in my

orientation class. All of them went on to become legends in the company and beyond. The core values were already in place, and the leaders walked us through them on our orientation day. I applaud the leaders who realized early on that they needed defined core values to guide their culture. They chose:

- Fanatical support in all we do.
- Embrace change for excellence.
- Results first: Substance over flash. (Note: throughout this book you will see me refer to these as separate core values. That is actually how we used them, and the company eventually separated them several years later)
- Keep our promises: Bad news first, full disclosure, no surprises.
- Passion for our work.
- Treat Rackers like friends and family.

I'll review all of these in-depth in the next chapter.

DEFINING YOUR CORE VALUES

I advise organizations to define their core values as early as humanly possible, even if they don't get them right. Once you hire your first paid employee or non-founder, you need to start writing down your mission and core values so that you can train people on their first day on the job. The joke I heard at Techstars is more truth than jest; it says, "The first time someone asks you if you have Memorial Day off, you are not a startup anymore." You need to have your core values—and employee orientation—already in place by the time that happens. Having new employees walk in and see the core values lived from day one helps create consistency in expectations and behavior.

The first step in defining your core values requires a lot of listening and fact-finding. Listen to your employees and customers and respond to them. David said, "Most core values will come from employees."

Ask yourself the following questions to begin thinking about your core values:

- What are the things that are important to you?
- What values will help you hire?
- What values help you fire?
- If you weren't present and an employee had to make a decision, how could they use a core value to make a good decision?
- How do you use a core value to celebrate a win when the value is done exceptionally?
- If the company asked you to train a new employee, what stories would you tell them that bring each core value to life?

DON'T CONFUSE YOUR EMPLOYEES

The bar is so low in business these days.

Core values are not the same as simply being a good human. Diversity, I would argue, is not a core value; neither is ethics nor honesty—any business should have those right from the start. You either value ethics or you don't. You would never start an Honesty Department. Whenever you try to introduce a belief system as a core value, it's confusing and very hard to manifest into real action by your employees.

Of course, there are exceptions to this. For example, in recent years, the hashtag #fakenews has created a lot of turmoil in the field of journalism. Because the brand of the industry is taking heat, a journalist can't afford to bend the truth or misrepresent even a single story. The stakes are too high. One false story and everything you do is now in question. So, if you are starting a news site or blog, having honesty as a core value would definitely be a plus *if you can make it real*. So, I'm not saying that belief systems never work, I am saying that they are the hardest values to make real and it is rare that I see them done well. So proceed with extreme caution.

Real core values can be measured, and it's hard to measure a belief system. How do you measure things like inclusiveness and honesty?

MEASURE AND CELEBRATE RESULTS

You might be familiar with the phrase, "what gets measured, gets managed." We need to measure the things we do, and most companies track metrics or data of some sort. If you're not sure where the goal line is, how do you know if you've ever scored a touchdown?

Core values shouldn't be lip service or simply words painted on a conference room wall; they should be actionable, measurable, and recognized when lived by employees. They give you an opportunity to point out what's being done and celebrate with the team when they're done well. I saw this core value in action at Rackspace time and again, where results were not only measured but celebrated.

Managers would say, "This guy literally stayed here all weekend migrating a customer's data from one server to another. Let's celebrate him." Or "This guy just hit 150 percent of his quota for three months in a row. Let's celebrate that."

CORE VALUES ARE UNIQUE TO COMPANIES

Not all companies have the same core values. As David Bryce said, culture is the personality of the company. You can have a company that has legitimate core values that it lives up to, which makes up its unique personality, and you may go in there and decide you don't like its personality.

I used to think that the military didn't have core values; they just bossed you around. Then I realized people in the military are absolutely valued members of a winning team on an inspiring mission. I just didn't like the personality, so it's not a culture I'd want to join. I don't like wearing a uniform, being told what to do, not being allowed to question things. It doesn't mean their core values aren't awesome and that their mission isn't inspiring, only that my personality doesn't mesh with the personality of the organization. There's nothing wrong with that.

MODERATION IS KEY

Can you get a core value wrong? Absolutely. Core values are more of an art than a science, and giving yourself the option to change them and the flexibility to change them is wise. You should remain open, but like everything, pursue changes with extreme care.

Too much of a good thing can be a bad thing. Every core value can be misused. Someone may do something borderline unethical because they wanted to get results. They wanted to sell the first million-dollar deal. That's where you need to monitor them, and that's why you have to have a strong leadership team committed to them. Otherwise, they may take a very dark path.

A good value can become a bad value at some point. A real core value can become a fake core value. All core values have a good and bad side.

BEWARE OF THE GOOD OLD DAYS

Employees who have been with a company for a long time will often give two types of feedback. They either pine for the good old days, which they view through rose-colored glasses, or they complain about former management and are glad things changed. Rarely do they talk about the reality; we did things that were good, but some things should have been changed, and we didn't change. Or, we moved away from things that were working.

The job of a leader is to objectively look at the past for examples you can learn from and apply to the decisions you are making right now and for the immediate future. My mentor Shannon Forester-Smykay once said, "Most employees will tend to romanticize the past even when it was bad." It is the leader who has the difficult task of discerning when to use the past and when to leave it there.

THE GOOD, THE BAD, AND THE UGLY OF FANATICAL SUPPORT

Graham Weston once said that there were two ideas that were worth a billion dollars of value each. The first one of them was *fanatical support*. The second was NPS.

THE UPSIDE OF FANATICAL SUPPORT

Shortly after David Bryce introduced *fanatical support*, the company noticed that it was also a point of differentiation for the company. At the time, Rackspace paid for servers at several of their competitors to evaluate their service. David remembers that one of their servers went down, and it took the competitor three weeks to give any type of response.

After that, Graham took $1 million out of the Rackspace marketing budget and gave it to David to hire more customer support staff.

Our customers wanted *fanatical support* from us. If our customers didn't care about customer service and we gave them *fanatical support*, it would have fallen flat and even made us look stupid. On the other hand, if customers wanted it and we promised to deliver it to them and failed, we would have damaged our brand by failing to live up to the promise. Success happened because our version of customer support collided perfectly with the customer's desires. Our customers were willing to pay extra AND we delivered on that promise of *fanatical support*. We embedded our customers' needs into our core value and that is why those two words are worth one billion dollars. How many core values out there do you know that are worth that much money?

HARD TO QUANTIFY

The bad part of this core value is that it's hard to quantify what *fanatical support* means and how you deliver it. What is fanatical to one person is normal or exaggerated to another. As we got bigger, people would weaponize it and try to manipulate people by using the core value. For example, a sales rep sells something completely crazy that the company doesn't do or can't support. When the customer service person pushes back and tells them that we can't do this, the sales rep fires back, "That's not very fanatical." A lot of times, fanatical meant saying *no* to protect the customers from a bad outcome. In the end, you can use it to mean whatever you want it to mean, and that is bad.

HERO CULTURE

The long-term effects of *fanatical support* were that we ended up putting too much value on the Superman heroics, such as a person staying all weekend to do something. And the ugly part of that is that we, as a company, became too dependent on superhuman acts to grow the company instead of developing long-term business processes.

We should have shifted at some point to telling people that it was more fanatical to create a system, process, or innovation that took away the need for someone to stay all weekend. In the end, we had so little automation that we struggled to scale as a company. And we ended up burning out many good people in the name of *fanatical support* because we never met them in the middle. We made heroic acts an everyday job expectation instead of a sporadic, rise-to-the-occasion event, which is the way it should have been. Shannon often said, "We are the firefighters but also the arsonists."

What ways have your teammates weaponized your core values to manipulate situations or promote bad behavior? And if they haven't yet, how could they?

COMMUNICATING A CULTURE

Core values nurture and feed your culture, keeping the immune system alive and well. You could tell your employees, "We've already covered the core values. We talked about it two years ago and the writing's (literally) on the wall. You should all be doing it." Someone who just joined the organization would feel like they're getting a crash course two years later. You want to live your core values and bring them up as often as you can.

Listen to the words. On a monthly basis, the Rackspace leadership hosted open book meetings, an early version of town hall or ask-me-anything meetings of today. If I took a transcript of every open book meeting that took place during my tenure, dumped it into a database, and pulled out the most commonly used words, you'd hear words like, "*fanatical support*, customer service, core values, delivering service" pop up again and again.

Culture is set at the top and drips down like ice cream melting on a cone. The things that are important to the leaders become important to the troops. During that magical time period at Rackspace, I rarely heard talk about our investors and board members. Leaders talked about our customers, *fanatical support*, and delivering on our goods.

THE STORY ALGORITHM

The best way to communicate your core values is through stories. It is the folklore of your company. As you will see in this book, I am going to give you a whole bunch of stories that brought our core values and culture to life. I think each core value operates like the Google algorithm. It's always learning, adapting, and getting smarter.

As your company grows, you will see employees do amazing and innovative things that reflect exciting interpretations of the core values. You need to write those stories down somewhere and keep them. It is the stories that help the culture spread. It is the stories that bringing meaning to each core value, and it is the stories that will be the best way to teach new employees how to behave. Stories will also be a good reminder for the employees that are already there but may have forgotten.

I believe that every company should keep a stockpile of stories for each core value. If someone doesn't understand them, you can keep dishing out more stories until it clicks in their brain. Also, if you don't have stories, then you need to create the ones that you would want to happen if the core values were lived out correctly.

These stories have to be so repeatable that your employees spread them amongst themselves. They are the stories that they tell at the water cooler, a cigarette break, or during lunchtime. If you can't tell your core value in a simple story, then chances are, your core value is not being lived out or it's a fake one. Either way, it's bad.

WRITE IT DOWN, KEEP IT ALIVE

A lot of companies believe so much in culture that they will create a role for someone to create it, fix it, or make sure it keeps going the way it should. While the intent is good, I think the tactic is wrong. Culture is everyone's job.

Rather than assign one person to manage culture, you need to write down your values and the stories that illustrate them. Then, put them somewhere every single employee can access in any given moment—a blog post, a book, a PowerPoint, but it must exist somewhere. I believe writing down your core values and stories is too important to relegate the responsibility to a culture manager. The CEO communicates and repeats the stories of your core values, so everyone sees what they look like when done well.

Zappos was the first company that I saw take their culture so seriously that their CEO, Tony Hsieh wrote a book about it. In *Delivering Happiness: A Path to Profits, Passion, and Purpose*, Hsieh shows how making culture a top priority led Zappos to success.

The founder of Patagonia, Yvon Chouinard, also wrote a great book titled, *Let My People Go Surfing: The Education of a Reluctant Businessman*. He talks about the experiences that shaped him, what led him to start Patagonia, and the principles that guide Patagonia's company culture.

Netflix achieved the highest standard of sharing their story when they created a living document—meaning they update it regularly—called "Netflix Culture: Freedom & Responsibility." Sheryl Sandberg once called it "the most important document ever to come out of the valley."

So, what's the point? Great companies and leaders record their values and stories. The even greater ones keep it alive and tend to it on an ongoing basis.

BUSINESS LESSON: THE CULTURE SCRIBE

If you are a small business, the CEO/founder is the keeper of the culture and writing these stories is critical. As your company grows and writing down stories goes beyond the CEO's bandwidth, hire someone with journalist tendencies to be your culture scribe. Their first job is to get the story told and then search high and low throughout your organization to find stories that exemplify the culture and write about them. This person reports to your CEO—that's how important it is. But never forget that the CEO is the chief champion for culture. If your company has amazing stories and your CEO never talks about them, no one else will either. They set the tone, always and forever.

SEPTEMBER 11

August and September of 2001 were big milestones for me in my life. My first day of work at Rackspace was August 6, and on September 29, I would finally turn twenty-one years old.

On September 11, 2001, I went into work like it was any old day. Back then, I would get to the office really early because I always felt behind on my work and I always wanted to get a jump on the day. I would boot up my computer and check the news while listening to voicemail and checking my customer tickets so I could triage what I needed to accomplish.

That day, just like usual, I fired up my web browser and turned it to CNN. Right there, on the front page, was a picture of the twin towers, and one of them had a gaping hole in it. The headline said that a plane had accidentally hit the tower. I looked up and said to my team, "A plane hit one of the twin towers."

My manager quickly fired back, "Bullshit." I said to her, "Don't believe me? It's on CNN."

As the entire world began to realize what was happening, something else happened that I wasn't prepared for: the entire internet started to slow down. The traffic on the web, specifically to news sites to find out what was happening, was through the roof.

I went into the break room to get a soda and a group of people were watching a TV. There was this feeling in the office that was a mixture of confusion and silent shock. Just as I walked in, we all witnessed the second plane hit the other tower. I ran back to my desk and checked CNN, but it was down. I went to five other news sites they were all down too.

I rushed over to the sales team and said, "Someone should call CNN and offer them free hosting to keep their site up."

"We are already on it," the sales rep told me, "but we can't get hold of anyone."

Thirty minutes later, CNN's site was back up. Only the twin tower story remained. Every story on the site had been removed, replaced by on single surreal white webpage with the CNN logo and one story.

Our own data center was across the street in the tallest building in downtown San Antonio. Paranoia overcame us as we thought of just how vulnerable it would be. When a crisis hits, you begin to think that anything can happen, and maybe our skyline was next.

On that same day, we officially opened a new part of our data center called Phase 3, which would handle all of our most complicated customers. As the account managers all walked across the street to the data center, I saw Graham Weston walk out of a restaurant near us. Although he was on the phone, he looked straight up to the top of his thirty-story building. I will never forget it. He had the look of someone who had never had to ponder what to do if a plane hit his building. I could see the wheels turning in his head, cell phone to his ear, staring up at the top floor as we walked past.

We visited Phase 3, but no one could focus on it. We only wanted to talk about what had just happened and what was going to happen. About an hour later, they sent us all home. I sat on the sofa at my brother's house and watched the news for what seemed like twelve hours nonstop.

The implications of 9/11 at work were huge for me. At the time, I had about a thousand customers that I was supposed to call and just check upon. We were assigned customers by region, and most of my customers were on the East Coast, many of them in New York. It felt so rude and insensitive to be calling people and saying, "Hey, how's your hosting? Anything I can help you with?"

In the end, I knew I needed to be proactive and see how they were doing. I had to see if there was any way Rackspace or I could help them. So, I picked up the phone and started dialing. As an account management team, we were driven by a desire to help and our core values to guide us.

After 9/11, ***embrace change for excellence*** meant *embrace change* because everything I knew about hosting was about to change. The business and internet world changed in one moment. After that day, we had to embrace change because everything HAD changed. Embrace change meant we had to adapt to the new world.

September 11 was the day the internet bubble burst, and for me, that meant churn. Lots and lots of **churn**. For those of you unfamiliar with that term, churn is also known as churn rate and it means the rate at which customers stop doing business with you. As I called through my list of customers, it felt like every other customer I talked to had to cancel their account. I learned very quickly that *fanatical support* meant doing the right thing for my customers. So many of them were in twelve- or twenty-four-month contracts, but when I called them post 9/11, many had gone out of business or were about to go out of business. *Fanatical support* meant doing the right thing and letting them out of their contracts without a fight.

These customers had bigger fish to fry and harassing them for a couple of months of hosting just seemed heartless and stupid. So, I didn't. I let them go. Our core values guided me to make that decision.

The churn was so bad after 9/11 that Rackspace rolled out a bonus that was pure triage. A normal bonus would say, if you make one more dollar than we lose, you get a bonus. This bonus plan was so radical that if we could just shrink the rate at which we were losing customers, we would get a bonus. Whoever heard of bonusing on negative growth? That's how bad it was.

The next core value that I used was ***treating people like friends and family***. Because most of my customers were on the East Coast, many of them knew someone who had died in the twin towers or someone that worked near the twin towers. For those customers, the best way I could ***treat them like friends and family*** was to listen. I must have spent days on the phone just listening to people tell me their stories, vent to me about the business, or shooting the breeze about anything because I was a willing and listening ear.

In the end, after everything had calmed down, the internet and the hosting world had been radically and permanently altered. The first big change was that fake businesses went under. Yes, like fake news is today, fake businesses were big business.

I had a customer that called me to churn. He had a simple static website for his soccer team. And ironically, he told me that a big cigarette company was sponsoring a banner ad on his website for $5k a month. As soon as 9/11 happened, they pulled their sponsorship and he was out of business. Truth is, he never had a real business to begin with. I was shocked by how many people had such flimsy business models, and I learned two very important principles:

1. Having a great company culture and solid core values helps you get through a crisis. It can actually make the company and the culture stronger.

2. Having a great company culture won't save you if your business isn't real.

STILL FANATICAL

Graham told me that after 9/11, the experts all told us we needed to stop using the word "fanatical" because it had developed a bad connotation. All the marketing gurus had stopped using that word. Then Graham went to a meeting where we had closed a big deal with a huge bank. When asked why the bank had chosen Rackspace, the first thing out of the CEO's mouth was, "Because of *fanatical support*. That's what we need." Graham showed that the gurus didn't know what they were talking about. *Fanatical support* was our secret sauce.

I learned the second lesson as I saw so many companies die in one day. Their culture did not matter because they weren't real companies but were instead pipe dreams. In the startup world, businesses often fall into the category of solutions looking for problems, or hobbies trying to be made into businesses. Either way, they are ideas that were never supported by enough paying customers to make them a viable business. A great culture can't save a fake business.

If you are an entrepreneur reading this book, make sure your business is viable first. Make sure the mission is not only something that inspires but is something that customers are willing to pay for. Otherwise, you are just one big crisis away from your own cigarette banner ad story.

A real core value passes the test of engagement—hire, fire, make decisions, celebrate wins, tell more stories. You either pass that test or you don't. Core values also set the tone for doing the work and working with others. As soon as I joined Rackspace, I got to see the core values in action. We'll explore just how in the next chapter.

KEY TAKEAWAYS

- Define your core values as soon as you can. Ask employees as they will often give you the best ones.
- A good core value can be used to determine who to hire, who to fire, and guide employees to make appropriate decisions in the absence of leadership.
- Decide early on the metric you'll use to measure your core value and communicate it to your team.
- Write down and share the stories that illustrate your core values; humans remember stories better than data points.
- Core values are driven from the top down; be the example of your core values every day in all you do in your leadership.
- Revisit your core values annually to make sure they still reflect who you are and what you want your organization to be.

Chapter 2

Applying Core Values to the Work

While David Bryce brought the idea of *fanatical support* to Rackspace, those of us on the customer support frontline had to figure out how to adapt it to our everyday tasks. Once *fanatical support* was established, all the other core values became clearer, and we could get creative and innovative on how those core values brought the mission to life.

RESULTS FIRST

Results came first, and the company did real things to get results. They tried things to see if they worked, and if not, they would embrace change again. That is part of the beauty of Rackspace.

When I got hired, all the account managers had a quota, but I would say it was like the Wild West—no law and order. Someone came and asked me, "Lorenzo, what do you think your quota should be?" In my head, I reached into a magic hat and pulled out the lowest quota I could come up with because I wasn't a very good sales guy. That's not how you want to run a business.

Then we hired Glenn Reinus, a man who was nothing short of a genius. Legend has it that before the hire, there were two candidates interested in leading our sales division. They both interviewed the sales team as part of their due diligence. The first candidate said, "Your entire sales team is terrible. I need to fire them and start from scratch." The second was Glenn and he said, "I can work with the team you have." Before he even got the job, Glenn was living our core values.

When Glenn joined the company, all sales reps were part of new sales. They closed all new business and then handed it over to customer support. We account managers then had to manage the customer account, sell to current customers, and manage all aspects of the customer until they left. It was a lot of work and not very efficient. Account managers handled all current customers, and at one point, I had close to a thousand customers assigned to me. We had a hard job because we were fighting retention while selling and putting out fires. We were the ones who took the brunt of the mess when customers were unhappy.

When Glenn interviewed with the executive team, one of them said, "I know sales are fluid. Sometimes you hit your quota, and sometimes you don't." Glenn responded, "No, no, no. I'm going to hit my quota every single month, and every single month we're going to raise the quota a little more."

The day Glenn was hired, he brought something that we didn't have: a system and playbook that he immediately and methodically started to roll out. He built a sales engine I've never seen equaled. Glenn created infrastructure and a whole book of rules of engagement detailing how to interact with customers and colleagues, and how to deal with disputes.

About the same time, there was a lot of confusion about the revenue being produced by the install base (current customers), which was being handled by the account managers. Some loved selling and closing deals. Other account managers, like me, didn't like the selling part, but really loved serving our customers. Glenn solved this problem by creating a new role parallel to account managers, called the business development consultant (BDC), who focused on upselling current customers. The company recognized the need to both grow revenue and manage—meaning reduce—churn. Account managers were split according to those who loved serving customers and would remain account managers, and those who were more inclined to sales would become BDCs.

I was one of the odd cases that they didn't know what to do with. My manager, Anne Bowman, knew that I loved serving customers, but Glenn, noticing that most of my friends were in sales, thought I should be a BDC. One day, when I was in the break room, Glenn came to visit with me and gauge my interest in sales. I was intimidated by him because of how smart and influential he was, and when he came to see me, he was accompanied by two sales leaders who I didn't know well at the time (we have long since become amazing friends). The two sales leaders were Matt Schatz and Jairo Romero, and both stood well above six feet tall. It felt like Don Corleone walking into the break room with his capos, Clemenza and Tessio. After our quick chat, Glenn could smell that I didn't have the killer instinct for sales and politely excused himself. He had his answer, and I would remain where I was best serving the company—as an account manager.

After that, I started referring to him as "The Don."

Our leadership team then paired up each business development consultant with an account manager, and they were assigned to the same accounts. One had a quota for revenue, and one had a churn quota. One sold to current customers, and one served those same customers. I was honored to act as a beta tester for this program. I was the account manager and my business development consultant was Vladimir Mata. We are still close friends to this day.

That one move was genius because it took all the pressure off me to sell and freed me up to put 100 percent of my effort into helping customers, which was what I was good at. I love customers and didn't want to carry a quota, so I was assigned a churn metric. I was responsible for decreasing the rate at which we were losing customers.

Vlad and I got together, and I listed all the things I hated to do in regard to selling. I told him that if he did those things, I'd do the rest. To sweeten the pot, I volunteered to do all of the medium- and low-level upgrades, ones that didn't require negotiation and that would happen anyway, that counted towards his quota. If a customer wanted to negotiate something heavy, I would let Vlad take care of it. We quickly sketched out a social contract (more about those in chapter 4) for this experiment based on all our core values and *fanatical support*, and our beta test became what the company rolled out for everyone, including globally.

We did this for a month or two and just crushed it. Suddenly the average revenue per customer started growing astronomically because the guy dedicated to selling sat next to me. I would pass customers interested in an upgrade to him and boom! His sales quota was set high and he hit it. Then he might pass an upset customer to me, so I would get on the phone and calm him down. I hit the churn quota.

The reason Glenn was able to sell this plan so effectively was because he was dedicated to serving the customers better. That was *fanatical support* and also a *results first* approach. We weren't doing it so he could do a political land grab and empire build. The results were so spectacular, they immediately and literally changed the entire business forever.

We began training our peers, and it became so effective that one day in an open book meeting, Lanham told the company that the install base, which comprised our current customers, was doing so well that if aliens came down and abducted the whole new sales team, the company would have still grown just from current customers. That's an awesome thing, a business owner's dream.

> ### BUSINESS LESSON: LOVE THE ONE YOU'RE WITH
>
> A former Racker left to lead the sales team of another hosting company. He asked the executives who of them was selling to their current customers, and they said, "We didn't know you could do that."
>
> So many businesses become obsessed with acquiring new customers that they forget about the ones they already have. This single move at Rackspace was revolutionary because of this one simple idea. If you serve the customers you already have well and treat them right, they will spend MORE money with you. The cherry on top is how good it is for marketing. The cost to market to and acquire a new customer is always astronomically high. Selling to current customers is the most inexpensive marketing that a company can do and it's almost always the most profitable. Go and do likewise.

The server-hosting market was fiercely competitive when I joined Rackspace in 2001. Everyone was trying to differentiate themselves by either having the lowest price or the fanciest hardware. Rackspace was a lean, scrappy organization led by innately innovative entrepreneurs in both our founders and leadership team. They lived the core values every day, driven first and foremost to always look for ways to improve the business and the employee experience, to *embrace change for excellence*.

EMBRACE CHANGE FOR EXCELLENCE

When I joined Rackspace as an account manager, we worked in an open space in secondhand cubicles Graham had purchased at auction when a local company went out of business. The cubicles were arranged like a call center, and even when we were seated at our desks, we could see over the low walls. Our voices overlapped, creating a scene and the noise level like the trading floor of the New York Stock Exchange—minus all the suits. We were organized in teams, but everyone performed as a lone wolf. Engineers would log in and work on customer support issues. Account managers would take phone calls. Billing would do their own thing and the unspoken rule was that everyone was to try and hide from the customers unless forced otherwise.

When something went wrong for a customer, the account manager was the one to make or take the dreaded phone call. It was difficult for me, as an account manager, to get help on complicated issues. If a customer's hard drive went down, I had to get an engineer on the phone to figure the problem out, then call the data center where the actual servers were located and schedule maintenance to replace the hard drive. My title was account manager, but my functions were those of a project manager or coordinator. No one was incentivized to help me or my customers, leading to a lot of frustration for all of us.

After I had been in support for a while, the customer support and operations leaders came up with one of the most game-changing ideas ever, borne out of one of David's experiences. David couldn't connect his all-in-one printer (printer, copier, fax machine) to his computer. He called the printer company, and after being on hold forever, they said, "Oh, you called printer support. You have an all-in-one printer, so you need to call all-in-one support." He called all-in-one support, and they said, "You have a Mac. You called all-in-one support for PCs. You need to call all-in-one support for Mac." In his frustration, he called Rackspace's IT support, and within ten minutes, an engineer helped him connect his printer. The company had organized their support around themselves, not the customer.

David didn't want Rackspace customers to have that kind of support experience. The leadership team began calling customers every week to check on them and ask what Rackspace could do better. On one of David's first calls, he spoke with a graphic designer in Louisiana who said, "I trade commodities for a living, and every time I call, I call Desk Number Nine. The person at Desk Number Nine knows everything about my account. I don't have to re-explain the issues. When I call Rackspace, I get a different person every time I call, and I have to explain everything all over again."

The customer support leadership then created **cross-functional teams** that were incentivized, metrics-wise, on the growth of the team as a mini-company. That meant when customers would call in, they would automatically be routed to their assigned team. And to make sure we never had a situation like David's printer story, we made sure every team was a one-stop shop. That meant having all the roles and expertise necessary to take care of whatever the customer threw at us. Customers got to know the engineers and would request to speak to the one who knew their situation.

I was on Team A. We were set up to work like a mini-company within the company. The team was comprised of an account manager (me), a business development consultant (the salesperson), three or four engineers, a billing rep, and a data backup specialist. Team A had around a thousand customers who generated in the neighborhood of $100,000 a month in revenue. My boss, Anne Bowman, explained to me that if you took that number and multiplied it by twelve, that was our run rate. Based on our run rate, team A was a $1.2 million a year business. My brain short-circuited. With one small finance lesson, Anne transformed twenty-year-old Lorenzo Gomez into the CEO of Team A. I had just been knighted, and from that moment, I felt like every single server that we managed was my server. It was my company. The entire support floor was rearranged so that everyone on a team could sit next to each other. Each team would then be given bonuses for performance at the end of the month, depending on whether the team/mini-company grew or not. If you sold more than you churned, everyone on the team got a bonus.

This change was so counterintuitive to the way most companies operate. In most companies, the person on the bottom of the totem pole or the lowest paid person is the one that they make talk to their customers. Our cross-functional teams took a bunch of salaried Rackers and made them our customers' personal IT support.

The day that plan rolled out, everything changed. In my entire career, I have never seen a change in people's attitudes as dramatic as that day. Engineers who you couldn't beg to help you the day before all of a sudden couldn't wait to get on the phone with me. Everyone became galvanized around helping our customers because there was a financial incentive. It was electrifying. I remember one engineer being on the phone and telling a customer, "Looks like your hard drive is getting pretty full. I really think you need to upgrade and get another one. I'm gonna pass you to our BDC so he can help you with that."

My jaw hit the floor. But after I picked it up, I knew the Rackspace *fanatical support* revolution had begun.

> ### BUSINESS LESSON: THE DELICATE DANCE OF CHANGE
>
> The truth is no one likes change. Don't believe me? Ask someone to move to a new desk twice in a month and see what happens. The problem with change, especially big change, is that you are fighting one of the strongest urges in human nature, which is to keep things the same. People guard the familiar like a junkyard dog. So when your company is growing fast, you are going to have to handle a massive amount of change and, as a result, lots of employee pain. The best thing to do is to overcommunicate the Why. You need to be prepared to explain, re-explain, and explain again. You also need to beware of change-fatigue. Change too much during a certain amount of time, and you will give your team whiplash. It's a delicate dance, but as a leader, you have to know when progress is worth the discomfort of change.

TEAM A IN ACTION

Prioritizing the customer experience was core to Team A's success.

I was once on the phone with an angry customer. Across our low cubicle walls, a legendary engineer named Jay Bridges heard me being chewed out and immediately gave me the look that said, "I'm logging into the server right now." He didn't say a word. We just exchanged glances while I told the customer, "I have an engineer logging on to your server this very second. I'm going to conference him into our call right now. We're going to work on this for you and get it back up." It stopped the customer dead in his tracks because they were used to going through the phone maze with tech companies. My teammate saw me in pain and said, "Uh-uh, we're Team A, and we're going to do this together."

I often hear people preaching that the new world will go 100 percent remote work from home. And although I do agree that more people should use it, I think it's nonsense to say that it applies to everyone. Jay seeing my pain and responding proactively is something you cannot do remotely. We were in the trenches together, and that was part of what fueled our success.

Team A was one of the highest-performing teams of all time. I'm proud that we dominated, and everybody took pride in the fact that our mini-company grew like crazy. I felt like a valued member of a winning team on an inspiring mission. Most people struggle with change, especially when it comes to their job and how they do their work. Rackspace's business was built on the ever-changing internet world and our primary core value, *embrace change for excellence*, reflected that. With the cross-functional teams, we changed our physical seats and were surrounded by people who did different jobs. We lost the departmental safety net to become that mini-company in the company. If you were a billing person, you no longer sat with your billing buddies but with an engineer, an account manager, and a sales guy. You were on your own, but on a team.

I love this story because when the business demanded it, we took the word "change" off the conference room wall and turned it into a real-life business win. It was radical and risky as hell, but we did it anyway—and it worked. That was the day *embrace change for excellence* became real for me.

What's your company's version of this? If you have that story, write it down and share it because that's how you spread your core values.

BUSINESS LESSON: WHAT MAKES A TEAM?

Lots of great literature has been written about teams and how to build a great team. The best quote I have found comes from the book *The Wisdom of Teams* by Jon R. Katzenbach and Douglas K. Smith. In their book they write, "All real teams share a commitment to their common purpose."

It's not the cool name that makes you a team. It's not the number of people you have or their skills. It's having a common purpose. Are you on a team? Make sure everyone around you knows what the common purpose is—then get ready to achieve great things.

ACT LIKE A LEADER

One of the most intimidating days of my life happened when I learned I'd be sharing a cubicle with Graham Weston. Someone from facilities came by and said, "Oh, Lorenzo, Graham doesn't want to be in an office anymore. He wants to be where the action is, and you have the only open cube. He's going to sit with you." Yikes. He showed up with the two or three people who help run his life and set up shop on the other half of my cube. He was in and out a lot, of course, doing chairman-y things. I expected someone with his authority and position to be a super aggressive leader who kept a watchful eye on you to make sure you weren't slacking off. Instead, I discovered a truly humble and genuine person. I once heard a preacher say that if you ever met a truly humble person, you wouldn't walk away and say, "Wow, that person was really humble," instead, you would leave and say, "That person was incredibly happy and really interested in me." Those words describe Graham Weston. When he was on the floor, he was truly interested in everything there was to know about you—not what you could do for him, but who you were as a person. He proved to be approachable, accessible, and caring toward employees and customers. I, and all the Rackers who saw Graham in action noticed that he was a visionary. Graham knew how to sell his ideas and he espoused the mission that we all wanted to follow.

Nobody is going to love your business as much as you do.

As a leader, putting yourself in the middle of the action where your employees are doing their tasks and facing their challenges may be one of the loudest ways to authentically share your enthusiasm. It shows that you want to know the people in the business, and you want them to be a part of it. It also shows them that the frontline of the work is not beneath you. The message that sends to your employees is greater than any blog post you can ever write.

One day I was on the phone with an angry, screaming customer whose website had gone down. He demanded to speak with the CEO. Graham, who was chairman and CEO at the time, was sitting next to me but could only hear that I was getting yelled at. He had this comforting, apologetic look in his eyes. I thought about the customer's request for a split second. There is no doubt in my mind that Graham would have jumped on the call if I had asked him to. But I wasn't going to do that. I was on Team A, damn it! And Team A was an autonomous high-performing team. We were a mini-company, and we could handle this problem ourselves. I told the customer our CEO was very busy and probably on a plane to an important meeting somewhere. I told them, "I am going to transfer you to my manager, who has the authority to help you with this situation." As I transferred the call, Graham whispered, "Great job." I knew we were cool from that day forward.

Another time, Graham was walking toward the elevator

with five or six guys in suits. They could have been board members or potential investors; he didn't say. He stopped me as I walked by and asked, "Lorenzo, how many customers do you have?" I said, "Five hundred." He then asked about my churn rate, what trends I was seeing as to why customers churned, and revenue from my customer base. Every question he asked, I rattled off the answer with confidence. I was thinking, is that all you got? What else? Ask me more and let me show these suits how well I know my business. He then thanked me and got on the elevator with the suits. I could tell he was pleased, but not as pleased as I was. I was living Rackspace like it was my business because that's the example he set.

OPEN BOOK

Lanham, our president, was a Harvard MBA, and every open book meeting was a masterclass on managing a fast-growing company. He had this amazing ability to explain complicated business concepts simply, so we understood how they affected our day-to-day jobs. Every single concept made sense to me except EBITDA. I still don't know what it means except that it's a finance term and it's important as hell. I loved listening and learning from him during open book. Lanham also took every opportunity to reinforce the important aspects of company culture. At one of the first open book meetings I attended, Lanham spoke about the importance of *fanatical support*. About fifty or sixty employees stood around or were perched on their work-spaces. Lanham said, "Raise your hand if you've called Time Warner lately." Close to fifty hands went up. He continued, "Now, keep your hand up if you actually spoke with a human being." All fifty hands went down, and everyone started laughing.

"We're going to be the company that answers the phone."

The laughter stopped. Lanham's message was that every other tech company hides from its customers. We were going to be the company that answers the phone every time. Not only were we going to answer the phone, we were going to help our customers and provide *fanatical support* every single time.

I was twenty. I'd never heard such a radical idea. I thought to myself, *"That is so punk rock, anti-establishment, sticking it to the man. Yeah!"* I loved it. Our customers loved it. Our salespeople could tell potential customers to call our competition and see if they answered the phone, and then come back to us.

I was on the front lines picking up the phone every time it rang, so Lanham was speaking to me and everyone else at the organization. He showed how each of us could contribute to the organization, and he made us feel like valued members of a winning team on a mission. We all felt the huge responsibility to give our customers the *fanatical support* that David Bryce had inspired.

Lanham gave us a specific tactic and a story to support the core value of *fanatical support* and he did it in front of the whole company at the open book meeting, so they knew it was important. He didn't simply say, "Deliver *fanatical support*. It's really important." Mic drop. He gave us a vivid example that each of us had lived in our own skin, which allowed us to relate to our customers and figure out ways to treat them the way we'd like to be treated as customers. Our core value was *fanatical support*, and the tactic was to pick up the phone every time.

From there, customer support grew. As an account management team, we looked for ways to continually improve our *fanatical support*. Our team kept a list of ways we could provide it. We also decided to respond to all customer emails proactively. This sounds pretty straight forward, yet it was anything but. Each one of us had hundreds of customers and being proactive while also having so many inbound requests felt impossible. However, everyone intuitively knew that there was nothing fanatical about being reactive only. If we saw a website was down, we would try to contact the customer and get it fixed before they even noticed the problem. In team meetings, we began to talk about what we were doing. I remember in one of our account manager meetings, one of the AMs showed us an email template she had written to help get customers to renew their contract. She had a crazy high response rate. After the meeting, she shared it with us, and we all started using it. If another team had a great tactic, the other teams wanted to do it, too. There was a healthy competition, but we all knew that we had to share what was working with everyone.

At one of the open book gatherings, Lanham and Graham explained the 80/20 Principle, *also known as* Pareto's Law, to explain how a few inputs equal maximum outputs. After analyzing our customer base, they realized that 20 percent of our customers accounted for 80 percent of our revenue. With the discovery of that insight, they wanted to create a higher-tier level of customer service focused on the 20 percent of the biggest customers. This newly formed team also focused on profiling these customers' needs so we could get more customers like them. Anne was asked to go run it along with some hand-picked support and salespeople. I felt like we were creating a Rackspace Navy Seal-type team and it was exciting to watch. The new division was called Rackspace Intensive. And as soon as it launched it started growing like crazy. We could have kissed Pareto on that genius Italian face of his. I wasn't part of the team, but the account manager who went there was one I had helped train. I saw my boss get promoted and get more responsibility because she demonstrated the core values. Like me, Anne hadn't graduated from college but was judged on her merit, not her credentials. I believed I could do the same.

LEADERS SET THE EXAMPLE

David Bryce said, "Efficiency is overrated when you compare it to return on customer."

During this time, we watched the leaders and founders of the company get on the phone with customers. One of the original three founders was Richard Yoo. He was a technical guru, and when I first started, he helped serve as a sales engineer for the account managers. I loved Richard because he was the first original founder I ever had a conversation with and he was so down-to-earth. He knew I didn't know anything technical, but he never made me feel stupid and was always willing to jump on the phone with a customer. I also loved that he used to ride around the office on a scooter. Legend.

One month in the spirit of playful, healthy competition, every senior executive and founder set a personal sales quota and took sales calls. My friend James told me that he loved hearing our co-chairman Morris Miller on the phone. Morris was a stone-cold closer and James loved working deals with him. They modeled the notion that they were not afraid to get dirty and help us help our customers. Great leaders, regardless of the size of the company, create a mechanism to actually hear what's going on and figure out what they can do even better.

Too many companies have an "us versus them" mentality when it comes to employees and leaders. They feel that the leaders are in their ivory tower and the subjects are doing their bidding, and that is not a healthy dynamic. At Rackspace, we felt like the leaders were advocates for us, the employees. Anne Bowman would go into every leadership meeting ready to do battle on behalf of every single account manager. I didn't know what those meetings were about, who was in them, or what the outcomes were, but I did know one thing: Anne went in on our behalf to get us more resources, more tools, and more money. Anne was one of the very first leaders who saw my potential and one day she pulled me into a conference room and said, "Lorenzo, you're a really hard worker, and I know you don't know what stock options or company shares are, but you deserve some and I'm going to give you some." She gave me two thousand shares of Rackspace stock. I was naïve; I didn't know anything about stock, but she knew that the stock was being fought over and went out of her way to educate me. She told me to hang onto it because it would be valuable one day. I didn't realize it at the time, but that single act was the most financially generous thing anyone had ever done for me up to that point in my life. That's not employee versus leader. That's your leader taking care of you.

The leaders of a company always set the tone. If your leader says you're all about *fanatical support*, yet you can never get them to meet a customer or call a customer, you might as well go back to surfing YouTube. Their words mean nothing without action.

The Power of Two

In *Power of 2: How to Make the Most of Your Partnerships at Work and in Life,* Rodd Wagner and Gale Muller talk about making the most of your work-life relationships. The book chronicles some of the greatest teams and dynamic duos and what made them powerful. Bill Hewlett and David Packard—founders of Hewlett-Packard—for instance, received equal pay so they would be on equal footing. Another founding team wrote a contract that if they ever got into a disagreement or they were at an impasse on a decision, they would flip a coin. Whoever won the coin toss would get to make the decision.

When we got our act together at Rackspace, there were no lone wolves. Even sales guys who carried individual quotas were placed on teams.

We are more powerful in twos and threes. I always say your team should be small enough to feed with two large pizzas. The Navy Seals operate on the famous "buddy system." Their smallest team unit is called a swim pair. Even though most of us don't work in life-or-death situations like the

Navy Seals, I believe there is a great lesson here for us all: You need to consider how the decisions you make affect the people around you. When you're on a team, you're constantly thinking about what is good for your customers and team members.

At the end of the first month after we'd rolled out our cross-functional teams, I was tasked with tallying the churn and revenue for our team. My teammate Jay Bridges, an engineer, called me on his day off, which was odd and unexpected. He asked about our net revenue (total revenue earned from sales minus our churn) and wanted to know if we were going to receive bonuses. He said, "We better bonus Lorenzo, I want to build a swimming pool in my backyard." That's when it hit me—we were all in this together! Lucky for him, we bonused big that month. It's hard to think only about yourself when the whole company operates on a team dynamic. We serve our customers better together.

Who's on your team? In today's gig economy workforce, even individual freelancers work on teams. As I am writing this book, I have an editor who will check my work. And she has an editor who will check both of us. We work remotely from different cities, but we are a team. Are you a freelance programmer who has someone QA your work? Then you are on a team, too. Few people truly work alone. It's important to identify what team you are on.

THE RACK STAR TRADITION

"Rack Star" was a very sales-centric tradition. In the sales culture at Rackspace, hitting your quota was just table stakes. It meant you got to keep your job. If you wanted to excel, get promoted, have ideas, or be listened to, you had to do better than 100 percent. The sales reps who delivered over 110 or 120 percent consistently for a quarter- or half-year got to go on Rack Star, which were these crazy extravagant parties for sales reps. They included all of the things you associate with sales parties.

It was so cool watching them get rewarded for being winners. You did not want to miss out on that Rack Star event. The sales team were all fierce competitors.

Glenn Reinus is one of the true heroes of Rackspace. He played a huge part in the level of success Rackspace reached, leading to the eventual IPO. He built a revenue machine none of us had ever seen before going public, and it worked because he understood how to do it and hire for it. His true brilliance was understanding that he needed to create a subculture. His leadership set a tone that was different from the rest of the organization but still operated within the boundaries of our core values and aligned with the company mission.

In hindsight, I understand why he created this subculture. Sales, in general, is highly competitive, yet the Rackspace culture wasn't, we were all about service delivery—*fanatical support*. Glenn needed to create a culture that stimulated healthy, super-duper crazy competition internally and toward Rackspace's competitors.

For example, from the first day I stepped off the elevator, I noticed that Rackspace had a techy relaxed dress code—lots of tattoos, shorts, and very few shoes. Over time I slowly traded my Ross Dress for Less polo for a t-shirt and my khaki Dockers for cargo shorts. But in Glenn's world, you came to work dressed for success. Everything mattered, from what the sales team wore and how they interacted with visiting clients to coming up with and presenting new ideas.

For example, he picked three guys he saw potential in and mentored them to be future Glenn Reinuses. He was methodical about their development. One by one, he sent them over to run the UK sales and get international experience. Then those guys had their own people that they trained. He had developed an infrastructure of people whom he had trained with a long-term vision. His understanding of what it took to build the sales culture was so big he could write a book about it.

I have no doubt as Glenn came up with ideas, he stored them in his brain to roll out at a future, appropriate date. He was a genius ahead of his time.

One of his tools was a living document he called "The Rules of Engagement," which outlined the most comprehensive social contract I've ever seen within an organization. It was a fifty-page document that outlined specific sales scenarios and situations and how to handle them. Leaders could reference it when there was a dispute to resolve or when they faced a situation they hadn't dealt with before. He was so intentional about his culture that he put in the time to analyze what worked and record the collective memory.

Every culture needs a living document like "The Rules of Engagement" to provide the same guidance that Glenn did to his sales team. As described in chapter 1, you must record your mission, values, and stories, so they can be referred to when decisions have to be made.

Glenn left shortly after Rackspace went public, but the culture he built was so solid that it endured years after he left. Over the years, I saw many hotshot executives join the company and try to tweak or improve Glenn's system, but all of them failed. To this day, I don't think anyone has ever come close to improving upon his system or the foundation he laid.

BUSINESS LESSON: TRADITIONS AND HEROES

Every company needs their own unique traditions that do these three things:

1. Celebrate the values you want everyone to live by.

2. Give the employees stories to remember those values.

3. Honor and acknowledge the heroes of those stories.

The Rackspace tradition of Rack Star celebrated the sales reps who not only hit their quota but exceeded it. During their celebrations, they would tell the organization the dramatic stories of the hard-fought deals and how they closed them. And then, one by one, they would celebrate the sales reps by name. It's the way your organization can point to specific people and say, "This person is a hero here, and you should aspire to live our values the way they did in this story."

What traditions do you have that do this?

"WHAT GETS MEASURED GETS MANAGED"[2]

When I started at Rackspace, I got assigned almost one thousand customers, a completely unmanageable load. To say I was giving them all *fanatical support* could not have been more untrue. One of my first assignments when I joined the company was to call all one thousand customers. Someone told me, "Lorenzo, we have noticed that when we talk to customers, they stay longer and don't churn. So, we want you to call all your customers." When we were divided

---

2   I first read this in Peter Drucker's book, *The Practice of Management*.

into teams, we started to refine and introduce more specific metrics to measure whether I was performing well or not, which was a way better strategy than just calling them for no reason.

The first and most important metric was churn. My job was to keep customers happy and loyal for as long as possible. I thought the sales guys had it the easiest when it came to measuring success because their job was simply black and white. You either hit your quota, or you didn't. Now you can also measure them on upgrades, profitability, and stuff like that, but their core metric was measured on hitting the quota. If I was going to lose a lot of customers that month, however, it would not reflect well on me. My world was more like golf. I needed to keep that number as low as humanly possible if I wanted to keep my job.

Putting us into teams improved this situation. I had my churn metric, but the goal of the team was to grow. Whereas before, the account managers and BDCs were a team, now growth was measured in net revenue of the team. For example, if I helped Vlad hit his quota of twenty-five thousand dollars but I churned twenty-six thousand dollars, then Team A shrank as a mini-company—there was no way in hell I was going to let that happen. I helped the sales guy hit his numbers, and he helped me save a customer if needed. I learned that the best leaders look at metrics as a guide, with the exception of sales. A good leader would look at an account manager's performance and say, "Your churn is really high, but your customer loyalty metrics are fantastic. The amount of return credits you're giving is really low, and your customer base is growing." You need metrics because people need to know what scoring a touchdown looks like on an individual level. Lazy leadership looks at a metric as purely pass/fail. In my world, a lazy manager would have just asked, "How many calls did you make?" and call it a day. Strong leaders know a discerning metric tells you a good part of the story. Your job is to interpret the full story either with that metric or others, plus your knowledge of the person and their job.

Without metrics, you have people exerting a tremendous amount of energy into tasks, but who knows whether those tasks are important and contributive to the company or not. Metrics allow you to connect an employee's tasks to the goals of the company. Good leadership is essential in setting and measuring qualified metrics. You have to give people the right metrics, look at them, and see what story they are telling you.

We measured *fanatical support* in a couple of ways. First, we asked the traditional question: are our customers staying and growing? There were metrics for new revenue, upgrades, downgrades, churn, and net revenue. Then Graham found NPS, which is the ultimate loyalty metric. NPS asks customers a simple question: on a scale of zero to ten, would you refer Rackspace to a friend or colleague? To remind you, Graham once said, "Two things are worth a billion dollars to Rackspace: *fanatical support* and NPS." NPS was the true measure of *fanatical support* and required our customers to put their reputation on the line. The nuanced, analytical tool gave us great insight into how the customers viewed us—I think of it as X-ray vision into our customer base.

SUBSTANCE OVER FLASH

When I was hired at Rackspace, we all sat in low cubicles. You could see everyone around you, even when you were seated, and hear what they were saying. The lack of privacy was very intimidating, but they had been a secondhand purchase from a company that had gone out of business. Some companies raised millions of dollars like we did and leased the fanciest space with the fanciest furniture, but not Graham Weston; he was going to use the stuff he got for next to nothing. Those cubicles ended up being more advantageous to our strategy as the team members could hear what was happening on phone calls and make eye contact with each other and come to the rescue when needed. Rackspace's philosophy was that if we closed a round of funding, it was better to invest it into two more Lorenzos and two more Vladimirs rather than costly furniture and gold-plated hard drives.

Graham and his family owned a thirty-story building, the

tallest commercial building in San Antonio. It was Class A office space, mostly occupied by the city's best lawyers. Graham converted an empty floor, which normally would have been used to charge the highest rent in town, into a data center. For those who have never seen one, a data center houses thousands of servers (computers) in a giant room kept at a cool fifty degrees. I laugh every time I imagine the exchange at the elevators each morning as lawyers in their three-piece suits coming to work cross paths with the Linux engineers, dressed in all black with t-shirts that said, "No, I will not fix your computer" ending their night shifts.

Rackspace started the year 2000 with $1.4 million in revenue, which skyrocketed to $12 million by the end of the same year. The executive team also approached Sequoia Capital that same year, one of the biggest venture capital (VC) investors in the world, and received funding from them. Sequoia placed four or five companies in one fund, and Rackspace was one of them. Another one was an obscure company named Google.

Being in the same portfolio as Google was one of the many lucky breaks we had. Lots of startups have VCs breathing down their necks waiting for that payback in their spreadsheet to materialize. Sequoia was hands-off with us because no matter what we did, they had already made a gazillion dollars on their Google investment.

Rackspace didn't raise $10 million to build a fancy building. We asked, "What do we have right now?" Rackspace had two relatively small data centers at the time. One in Graham's building and another in a building in a rough part of San Antonio. Rackspace then bought an amazing location in Dallas for our third data center. The original owners had paid something like $30 million for it and had gone belly up. We bought it for about $1 million. That's *substance over flash*.

We always looked at our competitors to see what they were doing, and all they ever talked about was the latest tech. Their servers and data centers were like the super-duper spaceship that had every bell and whistle that a tech geek could dream of. We, on the other hand, were using white box tower computers in our first data center and moving all our big scaling customers to a data center we bought at a fire sale. We kicked butt because flashy data centers and computers didn't matter to our customers. *Fanatical support* is what mattered. What I did as an account manager mattered. Our customers knew this too, and they rewarded us with more and more business. Even if they wanted to visit the data center, they weren't allowed to go into their server or even touch it. We had to keep it pristine. Because of that, having this year's model versus last year's model didn't matter to them. If you're the NFL (one of our customers back then), you just want to make sure your server and service is up twenty-four hours a day. Our competitors were trying to sell gold-plated hard drives as their differentiation.

But your gold-plated hard drive is going to go down eventually, and when it does, you're going to call for help, and they're going to hide from you. Then you will call me, and I am going to answer the phone and have a guy standing at your server in the data center before you hang up the phone. Because that's how we rolled at Rackspace.

Rather than compete on price like our competitors, we differentiated ourselves from the organization by offering support. It may sound like common sense today, but no one offered support like that back then.

KEEP OUR PROMISES: BAD NEWS FIRST, FULL DISCLOSURE, NO SURPRISES

Full disclosure and transparency were lived out by Rackspace showing the employees the financials every month. That was the most transparent move I've ever seen, and I've copied it ever since with every company I've been in.

We were also transparent with our customers.

THE GREAT DATA CENTER OUTAGE

In the year 2007, I went clinically insane and decided to run a full marathon—no one should have allowed me to run 26.2 miles in ninety-five-degree Texas heat on a Sunday, but I did it anyway. Halfway through my run, the phone that I carried in my camel pack started blowing up. I thought my team at Rackspace was texting encouraging messages for the marathon. *"How awesome,"* I thought. Three hours later when I finished, I looked at my phone, and it was blowing up because we had an outage. Part of the data center went down, and a bunch of our customers went down with it.

I moved my swollen feet as fast as I could to get to the office. The phones were ringing nonstop. Everybody was upset, but we were on top of the situation. We stayed late to calm customers down as the servers came back up. We came into work Monday and began dealing with the aftermath. We issued so many credits and refunds for downtime I thought I would never see a bonus ever again. My team was very effective and still on the job at 6 p.m. Monday, getting everything sorted out. We were feeling pretty good and about to wind down for the night when our VP, Taylor Rhodes (who later became CEO), came to me at 6:10 and had a very serious look on his face. He said, "A truck just hit the data center." I instantly fired back, "Fuck off." I waited for him to start laughing, not appreciating his bad joke after a trying twenty-four hours.

He didn't laugh.

A guy driving a truck had a diabetic seizure, passed out, hit the curb, went into the air, and hit the transformer powering our Dallas data center. Taylor and I stood silently and looked across the call center as an eerie silence took over the entire floor. Then, the phones just exploded. A sea of red blinking lights lit the room as every customer that was down realized it and called in at the same time. My team was one of the few still there, and we immediately ran back to our desks to answer the phones and braced for impact.

Whenever sales guys sold customers on how safe our data center was, they always talked about acts of God. If an act of God happens, we have this redundancy and that redundancy. Well, an act of God happened when that truck hit the transformer. We were frantically calling teams back into the office. My team was on the front line, taking all the bullets and getting screamed at. We'd thought the Sunday outage was bad; now we were dealing with the grandmother of all outages—all the backup generators, power supplies, and air chillers were failing.

I was managing a Linux team. One of my customers was a big airline company. The CEO wanted to eat my soul, he was so angry. I finally calmed him down, promising to make things right financially.

Then the Dallas power company said they had to get the truck driver out of the transformer because he was still alive, so they shut the power down for the whole block. As soon as they shut the power down, the entire data center went down, again.

Once they pulled him out of the transformer, we fired the data center back up, but the backup AC unit that cools the data center was not engineered to have that much of a power surge at once. The chillers would not turn on. We should have powered the data center back up in phases. Now we were firing servers back up and watching the chillers that were coming on and off. My lead engineer was an amazing guy named Kevin Holmes. He was logged in to the servers to monitor the temperature gauges. I didn't even know servers had temperate gauges. The temperature should be around fifty degrees or somewhere close to that. Kevin logged in and from another cubicle yelled out numbers that reminded me of a sinking submarine, "Servers at seventy degrees, eighty degrees, ninety degrees, hundred degrees. Servers down." Somebody called the data center, and one of the techs said, "Hey, these servers are smoking. We are running down the aisles, pulling power cords out to stop them from smoking. Otherwise, they are going to catch on fire."

Things were happening and changing so fast, I didn't even have the time to tell customers all the details and simply reassured them we were doing everything we could to get their data back up. The *entire* company came back to the office. We were glued to our phones. They brought in several hundred pizzas from Pizza Hut, so we wouldn't have to leave to eat. Recruiters who weren't on the phone circled the office with carts of water, soda, and candy to feed those of us on the phones. Everybody found a way to help. The whole sales force was on the phone with customers they'd sold to. All of the executives were there. In the midst of a corporate tragedy was one of the most magical moments I'd lived in my career: seeing the entire company come together.

TechCrunch was a customer of ours at the time. They ran a hilarious article with a headline: "Quick, Plug The Internet Back In: Major Rackspace Outage."[3] Graham, Lanham, and Lew were there too, and Lanham decided to take **bad news first** to the next level and post a video on YouTube explaining everything. Anyone on the phone with a customer could share that link with a note from our CEO about what happened. It wasn't all pretty: a UK customer was so angry he said the refund for the current month of hosting wasn't enough. Lanham literally told him, "You don't have to pay us until you feel like paying us."

Just like gold gets more refined when you put it in fire, the same thing happens to your core values in a crisis. If they are real and you live by them, they will shine like bright gold and come to life. That night, we were experiencing real-time *fanatical support*—to our customers, as well as the rest of the company providing *fanatical support* to us, *treating us like friends and family*, which means not leaving us hanging in a crisis. Then our CEO was living out

---

3   https://techcrunch.com/2007/11/12/quick-plug-the-internet-back-in-major-rackspace-outage/.

full disclosure while all of those other things were taking place. Our company was completely unified that night. There were no politics that night. No hidden agendas or jockeying for power. This catastrophe brought clarity. Our mission was clear, and everyone was rowing in the same direction with the same urgency and passion, the same helping attitude.

In *Influence: The Psychology of Persuasion,* Robert Cialdini writes about what happens when a group of people go through an intense shared experience. The bond they form is almost impossible to break and lasts a lifetime. That happened to every Racker in one night in 2007. The company lived their values that night. Everyone there was unified by the experience, just like when two Navy Seals who survive hell week together are bonded for life. It meant something to say, "I lived through the great data center outage of 2007."

PASSION FOR OUR WORK

Before you start thinking that Rackspace hit a bull's-eye with every core value, I want to set the record straight. Rackspace, like almost every company out there, missed the mark on lots of things, and one of them was this specific core value. This core value contains a great lesson that all companies need to learn: this core value is fake. It is utterly meaningless and here is how I know. Close to twenty years have passed and for every other core value, I vividly remember what they were and recall at least one story that brings them to life. This core value fails that test immediately.

Passion for our work: what does that even mean? Passion is subjective; how does it provide direction to employees on the front lines serving customers day-to-day? How is passion measured? And honestly, wouldn't every company want to say they are passionate about what they do? How does that core value help employees do their jobs or make decisions? The point is, it doesn't, and that is ok.

Most companies include one or two fallible core values. They fall into this trap because they think that is what people want to hear. What's not to like about being passionate? It's an aspiration, sure, but it's not a core value. If your company has a fake core value, I give you permission to kill it right now. Put a big red marker through it and have one less core value. Trust me, no one will notice, and it will also send the signal that your core values are more than just pretty words on the conference room walls.

TREAT FELLOW RACKERS LIKE FRIENDS AND FAMILY

Treat your friends and family the way you treat your fellow Rackers. That core value was powerful because we were a technology company in the early days when it was hard to find techies with people skills. Shannon used to famously say, "Hire for the heart, train for the skill."

We were trying to figure out how to create a culture from brilliant people who weren't used to working on teams, much less serving customers. Even today, you might be the smartest guy in the room, but you still need to *treat people like friends and family.*

One of my greatest insecurities at Rackspace was not knowing what everyone was talking about. Sometimes I could tell that the customers were annoyed that they were talking to me and I didn't know enough to give them a solid answer. They knew more about the internet than I did, and that made me feel insecure. We hired a sales engineer named Jeff Adams from one of our competitors. He was a cool guy whose technical knowledge was as much a part of him as his amazing dragon tattoo sleeve. Jeff started a weekly meeting to help all of us nontechnical people, a thing he called AM (account manager) Training.

Jeff's meeting became the most important meeting of my week. I didn't have to go to it, but I was dying to go to it—and I would have been stupid not to. I learned about all of the foundational concepts of the internet during Jeff's training. He had a beautiful way of explaining super complicated things—load balancers, DNS servers—things I could Google and still not figure out. Jeff had a genuine desire to help us be better at our jobs—no one asked him to do this. He didn't say, "Why don't any of these account managers understand how DNS caching works? It's not my job to teach them how the internet works." Instead, he lived out *fanatical support* and *treated us like friends and family*. He trained us gently and patiently, and never lorded his technical brilliance over us or made us feel stupid.

We had a third-shift employee who worked from ten o'clock at night to six in the morning, and he had cancer. He had used up his allotted sick time going to get treatment, so our head of HR asked if anybody wanted to volunteer and donate paid time off for him. People donating their time became a crazy spectacle, especially as Rackers tried to top each other in giving more time to him. It turned into this crazy auction-type frenzy where instead of bidding more money, people gave more of their PTO. One person said they'd donate a day, and someone said they'd give two days. One of our legendary data center techs, Roy Cortinez, finally threw down the hammer and gave him all four weeks of his PTO. That is what I like to call a *Friends and Family* mic drop. Many people didn't even know the guy with cancer, but there was such solidarity between employees they donated their time without question. Most people see a core value like *treating others like friends and family* and think it means saying good morning every day or being polite. Your core values have to be so real that they manifest into action. Real action.

On the downside, *treating others like friends and family* can be used as an accomplice for bad behavior. Early on, we had an absolutely brilliant engineer. But it turned out he had a pretty bad drug addiction, which was very erratic. On his highs, he would work for three days straight, eyes bloodshot, resolving customers' issues like a mad man. On his lows, he was very difficult to work with or simply didn't come in. His Racker friends and family felt the need to help him and let him take another unscheduled day off, which meant that the rest of his team suffered in picking up the slack. Yes, we cared about him, but there's a point where his behavior was intersecting with the team and customers. Where do you draw the line? He ended up getting into nefarious activities; I heard a rumor that he downloaded a list of undercover police officers to his personal hard drive—which sounded like the plot to a James Bond movie—and quit because the cops were looking for him.

You can neither choose nor eliminate family members, but employees are a different matter. I once heard Reed Hastings from Netflix make a compelling argument for not comparing employees to family members. He suggests that you treat employees like athletes in a professional sport.

Consider the NBA sports team analogy. You can be an amazing, loving, and caring person, but if you never score a point on the basketball court, there's no place for you on the team. I prefer to think of an organization as a team where players are recruited based on their potential and they may be "traded" when their performance lags or they don't fit with the culture. We are here to deliver results. It makes having healthy boundaries difficult when you blur the lines of family and work.

When you ***treat people like friends and family***, it has to go both ways. If it doesn't, that's cause for that person not to be part of the team anymore. If I'm the highest-performing team member, and I see that this person skipped work and is getting away with it, I will wonder why I should come in every day and give my best. Why should I when I have to pick up the other person's workload? There's a reason it's called a winning team and not a winning family; a winning team is tied to results.

Much like you don't get to choose your family members, you rarely get to choose your teammates. You can choose to work well with them all the same.

CURMUDGEONS VS. BRILLIANT JERKS

There's a phrase in the tech world called the brilliant jerk. The brilliant jerk is a super genius guy who knows everything but is torturous to be around. He will look down on colleagues for not knowing something. He will be difficult to work with or reluctant to help customers. The brilliant jerk spreads dissension and poison.

The curmudgeon is a different beast. I learned how to love

many curmudgeons at Rackspace. They knew everything about everything, and they knew it. They had the burden of knowledge. As soon as they were face-to-face with a customer, their bedside manner was remarkable.

The poison is the guy who doesn't know how to stop and subtly gives your customer attitude. He condescends without doing anything to help and contribute. Brilliant jerks bring about the slow decay of your culture, while the curmudgeon simply needs a good leader who can manage and understand their strengths...and who doesn't throw the baby out with the bathwater.

That said, a curmudgeon absolutely can become poison with a poor leader. A poor leader will see their rough edges and makes the call that they are a brilliant jerk. A good leader will look at how the curmudgeon interacts with the team and if he's helpful with the customers.

The curmudgeons at Rackspace wore spikes and scales on their outer shell, but when they dove into the customers, they were beloved by them. Customers would ask for them by name. As a teammate to a bunch of curmudgeons, I would tell them my first test was with customers. My second test was on how they were going to treat me as their teammate. Also, it can be difficult to tell the difference because both the brilliant jerk and the curmudgeon like to complain. While the curmudgeon is harmless, manageable complaining, the brilliant jerk's complaining is designed to cause discord. He wants to fuel feuds and ignite. If someone on the team is complaining, and you're not leading well, everybody will get sucked in, including the curmudgeon.

It's one of the great strokes of genius at Rackspace that they could find and keep curmudgeons who adhered to our core values. CliftonStrengths helped them do so.

FINDING YOUR STRENGTHS

There's a notion that you can focus on improving your weaknesses, but you're never going to be world-class at them. Rackspace wanted to be a strengths-based organization very early on and focus on the things we were good at and how they benefitted our customers. When the company was large enough to justify human resources types activities, they chose the CliftonStrengths (formerly known as StrengthsFinder) assessment as the psychometric test to provide employee insight.

When Graham learned about CliftonStrengths, he realized it was a game-changing tool that we needed to implement. Every employee had their top ten strengths identified and then posted in their cubicle, which immediately improved our interactions. Previously, we'd go to someone's cubicle, explain a situation and ask for help, then go back to our own cubicle and call them incompetent. With this new training,

I could go to someone's cubicle and immediately see their strengths posted, which told me something unique about them and also explained things about them that were just a mystery before. This also allowed us to immediately see where we had common ground. It felt great to know that someone cared about what you're good at, and it was awesome to see how that tied to the business.

For instance, an engineer might take a long time to get on the phone with a customer. But when I look at her strengths, I see she has strategic and communication. This tells me that this engineer spends time studying a customer before he or she gets on the phone, and once on the phone, they are going to communicate a lot to the customer. It all makes sense now. They are not dragging their feet; this behavior makes them special and explains why they are good at their job.

For example, my strengths are:

- Context—I will research everything there is to know about a customer and their issue.
- Restorative—I love problem-solving, and I believe I can figure out anything within reason.
- Activator—I want to start yesterday. I don't want to plan anymore.
- Positivity—I'm going to jump on this issue with a smile on my face.

- WOO—an acronym for "win others over." At the end of this issue, I'm going to win you back over to loving our company and me.

CliftonStrengths was a tactical homerun that transformed our interactions. Teammates became more united because we knew the makeup of each other's DNA. It also showed us something very important. It showed us where our teams were weak. CliftonStrengths has thirty-four total strengths and each of them is put into one of four quadrants. The quadrants are Execution, Influencing, Relationship Building, and Strategic Thinking. After we all took the assessment, we could instantly tell the teams that were lopsided and those teams that had a proper, diverse mix of strengths. For example, if you had a customer support team weighted toward strategic thinking strengths, then nothing would get done. It would be analysis paralysis. That team would need to add more people with execution strengths so that someone would actually do the work.

Graham once said in an interview, "It is totally ok for individuals to have weaknesses, but it is not ok for teams to have weaknesses."

Once you look at your team that way, it changes everything. I also think that looking at teams this way is the birthplace of true diversity.

Many years later, when we moved beyond the simply psychometric test and started doing hardcore CliftonStrengths training, there was a card that read, "Tell us how you like to receive praise." There are different forms of praise, and not everybody prefers the same form. For instance, if I do amazing work, I'd want the CEO of the company to send out a company-wide email saying I was amazing. But we had some curmudgeons who would never want such a thing done for them. For them, a gift certificate or private one-on-one praise was meaningful.

Part of *treating others like friends and family* meant learning to understand each other better, and that's where CliftonStrengths helped us up our game.

COMMIT TO YOUR KUNG FU

When you reach a certain size, most companies use some sort of psychometric or personality test to learn about their employees' strengths, weaknesses, and behaviors. I have beta tested other evaluation methods, such as DISC, Myers-Briggs, Insights, and Enneagram, among many others. A good friend of mine loves Enneagram and is always trying to get me to use it, while I was trying to sell her on Clifton-Strengths. I was concerned that I was being close-minded and stopped to think about why I didn't want to learn about other methods. Then I realized that these personality tests are like martial arts. There is Kung Fu, Jiu-Jitsu,

Taekwondo, etc. I had chosen CliftonStrengths as the one to commit to developing mastery over. I wanted to be a Kung Fu master, per se—to study only Kung Fu for the rest of my life and be world-class at it. The point is that as a company, it doesn't matter which method you use. One is not better than another, but you need to commit yourself to one of them and become world-class in the knowledge of it. Otherwise, you'll never have mastery of the tools.

My favorite quote from Bruce Lee is, "I fear not the man who has practiced ten thousand kicks once, but I fear the man who has practiced one kick ten thousand times."

When it comes to culture, don't fear the competitor that has tried and tested every single personality test. Fear the company who has picked one and trained every single employee on it ten thousand times.

It's easy to stay very superficial with these different kinds of profiling tests. We started organizing certain roles based on CliftonStrengths, and all of a sudden, when people were struggling, the question was not, "How do we get rid of them?" but "Are they playing to their strengths or not?" That's how you incorporate them into your core values and how you hire and fire, as well as how you *treat others like friends and family*. Look at strengths before treating anyone as an anonymous cog in the machine.

My own strengths would be put to the test when I was tapped to move from Rackspace's San Antonio headquarters to the London office.

KEY TAKEAWAYS

- Communicate your core values to all your employees through a living document that's updated regularly to demonstrate how the core values are lived and measured.
- Choose core values that you believe in and that support your business.
- Avoid core values that are hard to measure or don't pass the hire, fire, decision-making test.
- Psychometric tests can help you hire and manage people who are a good fit with your core values; choose one and learn it well.

Chapter 3

Spreading Culture Abroad

In 2002 I was given the opportunity to work in the UK office for a month. The account manager in London was taking a one-month holiday right when they were going to hire a second account manager because the sales team was closing new business faster than a single account manager could handle them. They needed someone to go manage all the UK customers and train the new account manager.

Some people might have heard, "Hey, Lorenzo, you're a great account manager and we want to reward you with an exciting international opportunity." Instead, and although they didn't say this to me, I heard: "And you're the only one with no wife, no kids, no house, no girlfriend or dog, so we're sending you." The truth was probably a combination of the two: I did have a transferable skill set, and I didn't have complicated personal ties to San Antonio at the time.

In addition to needing a second account manager, I heard that the company was sending an engineer named Chris Hill, aka Chill over to help out the UK customer support staff, too. So, I begged them to put me on the same flight with him because up until this point in my life, I had only ever been on a plane once and was terrified of traveling internationally. True to his name, Chill was a cool guy and helped me get over my fear of not knowing what to do while traveling. I'd never even seen a subway before, and the number of new experiences was overwhelming. It was awesome to have someone to explore London with and Chill was a great travel buddy.

The UK office was made up of about ten or twelve people housed in a super small office space. What made it cool, though, was that our tiny office was inside the actual data center, across the street from Heathrow Airport. Every day around 10:30, the Concorde would take off and set off all the car alarms on the road next to it. For those that don't know—or are too young to remember—the Concorde was the fastest commercial airplane on the planet; it could travel from London to New York in three hours. Whenever it took off, one of the UK sales guys repeatedly pointed out that it was a British invention. I guess he felt like part of the national British aerospace winning team. (For the record, the Concorde stopped flying a year after my visit—although I had nothing to do with it.)

I sat next to the managing director, which is like the CEO of the London office, a true leadership legend named Dominic "Dom" Monkhouse. My positivity and Win Others Over (WOO) strengths easily came out during that visit. My desk was next to Dom's, and I learned very quickly that the English have a great sense of humor and love to banter back and forth. From the moment I opened my laptop, we got on like a house on fire, as they say. Dom and I loved critiquing the famous email scam where the Nigerian Prince sends you a message saying that he has twelve million dollars (or British pounds) and he just needs your bank account number to transfer the money. When my month in the UK was done, Dom bought me a t-shirt with the entire Nigerian email scam printed on it and also asked me to come to London full-time. He said they'd get me a five-year visa. I turned him down several times. I was young and scared to leave my family and the familiarity of my city. I also loved my Rackspace team, and it's hard to leave the winning team when you're on top of your game. And Team A was on top of the game.

My friend Jake Gracia convinced me that it was a once-in-a-lifetime opportunity that I needed to seize. Jake was like a big sister and one of the first well-traveled, global citizens I ever met. She was from Chicago, had lived in Italy for a while, and worked in New York. Because of her experience, her opinion and insight carried immense weight with me. I decided Jake was right, and I went. The timing was beautiful because the UK was scheduled to roll out the cross-functional team program, and I was going there to show them what had worked well.

Team A continued to be the best performing team in Rackspace customer service. After I moved to London, Team A received an award for having the lowest turn consistently in the entire company. I was proud of that because I knew that I greatly contributed to Team A's success.

WAVE YOUR FLAG

Before I left Texas, my best friend Dax Moreno planned a surprise going-away party and gave me an awesome parting gift: he bought a Texas flag and asked everyone in the US office to sign it—Graham, Lanham, the Team A members, everyone. I cherished the flag and was reminded of their thoughtfulness and my tribe back home every time I looked at it.

Then I packed my bags, got on a plane, and ten hours later, was in London. Other than visiting Mexico and Laredo in my childhood, I'd barely ever left the thirteen-block radius around my house in San Antonio. London was overwhelming, to say the least.

Texas had three, maybe four types of ethnicity: the white folks, the black folks, the brown folks like me, and maybe a few Asian folks. London was global. I instantly had new colleagues from Norway, South Africa, Australia, Zimbabwe, Austria, Ireland, and every other place I had forgotten since geography class. We think of the US as a melting pot, but that's BS. In London, every person I met was from somewhere else—and I loved it. My colleagues were used to working with people from different European countries or different continents, but I'd never experienced anything like it.

The managing director, Dom, instilled cross-cultural sharing. Whenever someone new joined the staff, he asked them to complete a list titled, "Ten Things You Don't Know About Me," along with a funny photo of themselves, and hang it on a corkboard near the break room. For example, a Norwegian named Jon Andersson wrote that his hometown is above the Arctic Circle, that he spoke four languages, and had never driven a car—I thought he was so cool and smart and wanted to be his friend. An Australian guy who I trained wrote that his grandmother had survived the Titanic. What the what?! And yet another wrote that he used to control satellites for the European space station. The background of each person was astounding. I wanted to steal each and every list, mail them to my mom and tell her, "Look at the cool people I get to work with!"

Shortly after I arrived, the UK office decided to enter the

Sunday Times' annual Best Companies to Work For. Dom appointed my man-crush Jon Andersson to put together the contest entry that focused on our culture. Jon came by my desk and asked me if I had any ideas for our entry as evidence for why Rackspace was the best place to work.

I said that I'd just gotten there but I'd noticed that everybody is from a different country, which I thought was cool. I said, "Maybe each person can display something that shows where they're from." Jon said, "That's a great idea." He went off to collect other ideas, but I continued to think about it. We were already sitting in cross-functional teams; the other account manager and both BDCs were all British women.

I silently decided I was simply going to do it. The next day I brought the Texas flag that Dax had given me, and I hung it from the ceiling tiles. I didn't know it at the time, but just like that, a tradition had been born.

I soon found out that one of my engineers, a South African guy named Mike Petrie, had overheard my idea the day before. As soon as I hung my flag up, Mike Petrie reached into his bag and pulled out the South African flag. And for one glorious day, two former colonies of Great Britain were proudly hanging their flag deep in the heart of the empire.

The English women on my team were not about to let that

stand, and all three of them ordered their own English flag of St. George—with overnight delivery! Pretty soon, people were ordering their country's flag from Amazon and hanging it from the ceiling tiles too. The British folks hung flags from their county or town. Dom liked the idea so much that he asked each person to hang their country's flag over their desk.

By this time, the Rackspace office had about a hundred people and was in a larger office space. It had grown from the tiny ten-person UK office to a full-blown international Europe, Middle East, and Africa (EMEA) office. But when you walked into our office and saw a hundred flags displaying all the different colors and styles of the globe, it was a sight to behold. A few weeks later, the landlord came by and said we had to take the flags down because they blocked the sprinklers, creating a safety hazard. Dom refused. No way were we taking our flags down!

The flags were a great conversation starter. A fellow Racker from Austria, Thomas, was a pretty friendly sales guy, so I walked over to his desk and asked him to tell me about the eagle on his flag. "Oh, Lorenzo!," he said with an accent that reminded me of Arnold Schwarzenegger, "It's the Steinadler! The Steinadler is the Austrian eagle. He's much smaller than the North American bald eagle, but he's faster and soars in the Alps! He stood up and repeated himself, "He's smaller, much smaller, but faster, much faster," and spread his arms like an eagle, proud that the Steinadler was faster than the US symbol of life, liberty, and the pursuit of happiness.

I realized that day that everyone is proud of where they come from. Everyone sees their home country as a *winning team* even if the rest of the world doesn't. When I asked someone about their flag, I might know they come from a war-torn, dictator-led country that's suffered genocidal massacres, but they would say, "We have a terrible leader right now, but we grow the best strawberries in the world." The flags reminded each of us of what was good about where we came from and we shared that with each other. Hanging our flags made us feel like *valued members*.

Everybody wants to be proud of where they came from. And nothing says valued member more than a company celebrating who you are and where you come from. This acknowledgment made the flags special. You could be from a war-torn country, led by an evil dictator, but none of that mattered. Rackspace EMEA said we are proud to have you here regardless of where you come from. We are on the same mission. Now hang up your flag, so we can acknowledge and celebrate you. This is the difference between telling people they are valued and showing them. We took the value off the conference room wall and literally hung it over our heads for the whole world to see.

So, I ask you, how does your company do this? What do you do to show people by actions, not words, that you value them?

Later that same year, my old boss from San Antonio, Anne Bowman, came to the UK, saw the flags, and said, "We're going to do this back home." She was from Colorado, so as soon as she got back to Texas headquarters, she hung a Colorado flag above her desk, then someone on her team hung their Texas A&M flag. In the US, the tradition took on a different flavor as people hung flags from either their country of origin, the university they attended, or the state they were from.

When I left the UK a couple of years later, they asked if they could keep my Texas flag and frame it. In exchange, my UK boss gave me the St. George flag and had everyone in the UK office sign it. Eventually, Rackspace would officially adopt the flag as one of its traditions and when an employee had worked at the company for five years, they would give you a Rackspace flag. I did not set out to create a global company tradition, but that is exactly what happened. And to this day, it is one of my proudest contributions to the culture of Rackspace.

A HARD TRUTH ABOUT DIVERSITY

Diversity is about ideas and skills, not about fair representation. The good news is, when you do it well, it automatically hits both of them. One of the unintended benefits of the flag story was that for the first time in my career, I was given a very real and very different definition of what diversity at work looks like. In today's work culture, all too often, we define diversity only in terms of race and gender. I believe this is too limiting and overlooks a different type of diversity. Don't get me wrong; I am not saying that we don't need to hire underrepresented people because we absolutely do. But I *also* believe that this issue is more complicated than race and gender. Our EMEA office experienced the most amazing diversity I have ever seen in my career.

When people come from different parts of the globe, the differences aren't limited to the color of their skin. People who come from different countries cannot help but think differently than someone from another country. It doesn't mean you don't agree on issues. It just means they think differently about those issues because of the culture and context of their home country. In the EMEA office, they interview for all of the same roles and jobs we had in the US, but the pool of ideas and skills was diverse because of the diversity of the employees. Someone from South Africa who qualifies for the account manager job is coming from a country that not too long ago experienced the pain of apartheid. They have a very different view of the world when it comes to things like equality, fairness, and social justice. And because their ideas had been influenced by that experience, Rackspace EMEA was so much better by having them on board. Why? Because they were able to bring those experiences into Rackspace and merge them with our culture. As long as they signed up for our mission and operated within the core values, their diverse ideas and skills were welcome. Lanham, Graham, and Lew held to a great maxim spoken of by Marc Andreessen in an interview he did with Tim Ferriss, which is, "Strong opinions loosely held." They were also smart in letting the best idea win and discarding their ideas in the presence of a better one. We ended up with the benefit of so many radically amazing ideas because the pool was better. We weren't just trying to hire the same people for every job.

When I moved to the UK, I sat next to an amazing guy named Shoab. He was one of the highest level engineers we had in the UK and only worked on the biggest and most complicated customers. Shoab was also the very first Muslim I had ever met in my life. Coming from South Texas, where almost everyone I knew was a Christian Hispanic, I was curious to expand my world view. My first month in the UK, he invited me to dinner because he could see that I didn't have any friends yet. We ate amazing food, talked about Islam, the Old Testament, King David, gangster rap, and 2Pac. It's one of the most memorable nights of my life; I had the privilege to meet someone so different from me because Rackspace hired for real diversity of talent and perspective. Rackspace did not hire Shoab because he was

Muslim, they hired him because he was the best enterprise engineer who applied for the job who was also in alignment with our core values. He just happened to be Muslim. It was about skills and ideas first.

The core values were the driving force behind hiring decisions—as they should be—and the London office did a great job of screening candidates for matching value. They didn't care what country you were from or what your pedigree was. If you were down with *fanatical support*, *full disclosure*, and *embraced change for excellence*, you could fit in. It gave them a beautiful hodgepodge of people—a level of diversity I've never seen equaled. They didn't have a checklist saying they needed another woman, or a minority, or a person of color. They simply screened for job function first, then core values and our mission. This resulted in a beautiful diversity.

The reason you hire for diversity of ideas and skills is because no one will ever win the discrimination Olympics. No one will ever get the gold medal because you have to choose. What's more important? Women? Minorities? Uneducated Hispanic males from the inner city (that's me)? African Americans? Even African-American men and women are two different categories that both have hugely powerful associations with them. You're forced to pick one gold medalist, and you can't do it in business. Everyone can make a case to win the discrimination Olympics, but in the end, everyone loses.

BUSINESS LESSON: THE DIVERSITY FAKE OUT

All too often, when a company is feeling the pressure for their lack of diversity, the CEO will create a role for it, like chief diversity officer or something similar. In theory, it makes sense because it allows the CEO to tell people, "Look, we are dedicating real resources to this issue."

The bad side of this move is that it also allows the CEO to not make any real systemic changes while still looking like they are trying. When the entire leadership team and board of directors are all old white guys, the CEO can point to the chief diversity officer and say they are still committed to the cause.

Remember, you can create all the roles you want, but the leader always sets the tone. If the leader doesn't value diversity, then no one underneath them has any incentive to act differently—you need only look at the Our Team page on a company website to see how diverse, or not, a company is. I'm not saying that creating the role is bad, but creating a role without the CEO also leading by example will just be lip service and a waste of a good salary.

DIVERSITY OF DIVERSITY

The UK was able to harness the diversity of *region* and *country* which automatically introduced diversity of *religion*, *race*, and *culture*. This is what the flags represented.

When the customer support leaders created the first cross-functional teams, it was a type of diversity that no one had ever seen before. Having all those different *roles*, *skills*, and *job functions* showed everyone that diversity of skill is what would help our customers succeed the most and, as a result, help the company succeed.

When Graham said, "It's not ok for teams to have weaknesses," he was able to use CliftonStrengths to help bring diversity of *strengths* to each and every team in the company.

When it comes to writing a hit TV comedy show, Tina Fey writes in her book *Bossypants*, "When hiring, mix Harvard nerds with Chicago improvisers and stir." She intuitively knew that to make great comedy, you needed diversity of *education* and *street smarts*.

What are the other categories of diversity that you or your company uses to hire great talent? Once you tap into these other categories and stop limiting yourself, your team will become hard to beat.

LONDON EMBRACES CHANGE

Early on at Rackspace, there were visions and fantasies of going public fast because that's what startups were doing in those days. One of the checklists of going public was to have an international office. So, Rackspace set out to become a "big boy company" so they could go public.

The first going-public initiative completely failed, but the one or two people they hired in London were so good that they could keep the office afloat and proved its value. It was a testament to the people of the London office that they were contributing and growing so much they didn't have to shut it down.

The London office's strength was its ability to **embrace change for excellence.** In any remote office, there is an urge to say that the mother ship is so far removed that they don't know what they're talking about. They don't get it. Employees in the UK certainly had that sentiment at times (and for good reason), but their leadership did a good job of picking their battles with headquarters.

I saw London employees live the Rackspace core values every day, each in their own way. Whenever they were struggling, they used the core values to resolve their issues.

THE CHOCOLATE CAKE CLOSE

At the very end of my month-long stint in London, the office hired another account manager, Samantha, aka Sam, and sent her to the US to meet everyone in the office here. Sam was a larger-than-life, super-positive person, born to interact with customers. I was very eager to repay the UK kindness. I jumped at the opportunity to help train her and show her around the San Antonio office—but more importantly, my mission was to introduce her to breakfast tacos and for her to eat a Texas steak.

When I returned to London to work full-time, Sam was my main point of contact because her role in London was the same as mine in the US. She had a beautiful heart for customers.

For example, because the London office was so close to Heathrow, they had a much higher frequency of in-person visits than the San Antonio office. If a customer was coming to visit, Sam would say, "I'm going to make my famous chocolate cake." That was her way of bringing the **treat others like friends and family** value to our customer base. The funny thing was, nine months or a year into it, the sales reps noticed that 95 to 100 percent of the time Sam brought cake, they closed the deal. We started referring to it as the "chocolate cake close."

TRANSATLANTIC CORE VALUES

The London office was much smaller than ours, but their commitment to **fanatical support** would rival the US any day of the week. At any given moment, all of the phones would be ringing. Everyone pitched in routing the calls, which meant that everybody was responsible. In most offices, specific people were responsible to answer and screen calls. In London, those roles existed, but if those people were busy, everyone else was tasked with picking up that phone. They lived by the rule: don't let the phone ring twice if you can help it.

I thought the US had a big talent pool to cull from, given the population. London, however, seemed to have an even bigger pool and it was international. I had never met so many brilliant young people from different countries. Even across the Atlantic Ocean, the core values were so strong that they were actually living them with the same level of intensity that the US employees were. I took it for granted then that anyone who worked for Rackspace embraced the core values, but looking back, I see how unique and unusual that was. Most satellite offices develop values of their own—a localized version of the core values—even if they toe the line of the organization's core values. This is a true test of the strength of your values. If you have wimpy core values, you couldn't get a bunch of people on another continent to live them, much less with the same intensity with which the EMEA headquarters is doing it.

I admired the way the London office lived our core values in their own unique way, with subtle differences. You can tell if your core values are real if you listen to the front-line employees and they actually talk about them. After I arrived, I knew core values had made the transatlantic trip because the EMEA team talked about them just like we did in the US, only they did it in about ten different accents.

WHAT'S A YOUTUBE?

Throughout Rackspace, one part of our *full disclosure* core value was that anybody could see the revenue numbers. Because sales and customer service were so intimate and linked, I would check them all the time. I noticed a customer who seemingly came out of nowhere. They started small, then they doubled and then doubled again, and then they tripled and quadrupled.

Back in the US, remember, Sequoia Capital had invested in Rackspace (as well as Google, and later Uber and Slack). They were prolific then and still today arguably the top venture capitalist in the country. Graham's contact from Sequoia called him one day and said, "We just funded this company called YouTube, and they need ten servers online overnight." Graham was happy to help. They threw up ten servers for YouTube in our tiny little data center in downtown San Antonio, and internet history was made.

I remember the first time I read their name on the revenue report I thought, *What's a youtube?* When I looked them up and saw they did video, my next thought was, *These guys will never win this market; there are too many competitors.* Famous last words.

While YouTube doubled and tripled their revenue, they were growing so fast and had so many cease-and-desist letters for pirated content that Rackspace hired a full-time lawyer, at YouTube's expense, to handle all of the complaints. Because they used up all of the bandwidth in

San Antonio, we had to get more bandwidth. Very soon they were using more bandwidth than the entire country of France used in a month. In eighteen months, YouTube went from zero to being acquired by Google for 1.2 billion dollars.

One of the London customers offered a similar service as YouTube but with one main difference. While YouTube was open-platform, meaning you could put whatever you wanted online, this company curated the best videos for you. As a young man, it fascinated me to see how YouTube's one innovation—open source—led to a ginormous company. They literally came out of nowhere and burst onto the scene as one of the most important web tools in the history of the internet.

Everyone at Rackspace, including myself, who had nothing to do with their account, swelled with pride that the mission we were on was so inspiring that we had helped contribute to the birth of one of the most important internet companies of our time. It was a winning team top to bottom. Sequoia was the VC winning team that invested in us. We were the number one managed hosting company powered by *fanatical support*. And because of that we were able, in our own small way, to help enable another winning team, YouTube. Then they were bought by another winning team, Google. So, what's my point? It's the law of attraction: when you assemble a winning team, you raise the standard for everyone—your employees, your investors, even your customers.

So, or are you on a winning team? If not, you have a problem.

Even from a distance, I felt pride in the customers we served. That pride swelled when our service hit closer to home.

NEVER LOSE YOUR HUMANITY

I was in the UK when I read news about Hurricane Katrina coming. I watched and tracked its trajectory from London. I watched it slam into the Gulf of Mexico, near where I was from. When it hit, the mayor of San Antonio called Graham and asked him to help out. Graham owned an empty Montgomery Ward store that was part of a mall (that later became Rackspace headquarters) that was quickly converted into a shelter for hurricane victims. From London, we watched the San Antonio office help refugees on buses and create what the *New York Times* called the "Hilton of Shelters."

They brought in clowns to play with the kids. They brought in barbers. Rackers took shifts from work to volunteer at the shelter, sorting out bags of personal hygiene items and handing them out. They even created a database that helped people find lost relatives and then ended up donating the software to the Red Cross because it was so useful. We were an internet company, but we had not lost our humanity. We could practice *fanatical support* and still practice *treating others like friends and family* values to people who were in trouble.

The mission of Rackspace, to be one of the world's greatest service companies, was lived out with a slight deviation that day. We served refugees in the same way we served customers, with a big old wheel barrel of *fanatical support*.

Every person involved walked around with their chest out and head high. People want to believe that their company isn't a ruthless, profit-at-all-costs machine. Unfortunately, that is the brand of corporate America. We saw firsthand how you could call a timeout and help humanity. The hurricane hit only a three-hour drive from San Antonio, so everyone could easily imagine themselves and their families experiencing what the people of New Orleans experienced.

> ## BUSINESS LESSON: CULTURE REQUIRES CONSTANT WORK
>
> When your culture is firing on all cylinders, the highs are high, and the lows are low. In that way, your culture is like any other relationship, which means it requires constant work. Culture is never a set it and forget it. Everyone owns it and it's everyone's responsibility. And when you stop nurturing it, that is when the slow decline starts to happen.

We all felt like valued members of a winning team on an inspiring mission. When one of the three pieces is lacking, problems occur.

THE MOST UNHAPPY EMPLOYEE

During my time in the UK, I did about a six-month stint in new sales. I was terrible. I never hit my quota once in those six months. Normally you fire someone who doesn't hit their quota. My manager, an amazing guy named Andrew Gibbens, came to me one day and said we needed to have a talk. I thought he was going to hand me my P45, which is UK slang for getting fired. Instead, he shocked me and said he wanted to talk about my top five strengths.

Andrew pointed out that every one of my strengths helps me to serve customers better than anyone else. I wasn't winning in sales, so he put me back into a role where I am world-class. He had every reason to fire me, but he used my strengths and said, "Our company is better when Lorenzo is using his strengths to serve our customers."

My manager's wisdom and discernment took Clifton-Strengths from being something we said we valued at Rackspace to making a strategic company decision based on it. That's how you do it for real. I was so grateful for Andrew's move. I was back in a role where at least I knew I was adding value to the company again. But even despite changing roles, I was unsatisfied.

When I went to the UK as a young man, I was very naïve and negotiated a terrible salary. The head of support told me that they needed to do a cost-of-living adjustment for me to come over. I was about to be living in one of the most expensive cities in the world, and instead of adjusting my salary up, they adjusted it down. He said that the British pound was valued more than the dollar and because of that, they needed to take my salary down. So I would be going from $30K US dollars to 20K GBP (British pound). Knowing what I know now, it doesn't make any sense because if an apple costs $1 in the US it costs 1GPB in the UK, so you need to make the same amount for cost of living. The value of what it converts to doesn't matter. I was so ignorant of negotiating an international salary that I just agreed to it. I also did it because I believed in the core values and I trusted that they would be doing the right thing. Bad move on my part.

I struggled to make ends meet, and I can say without being dramatic that it was the poorest I have ever felt living on my own. When it finally hit me what they did, I felt so hurt and betrayed by them. It was the opposite of what I thought our *treat others like friends and family* value meant. Whenever I brought up my situation with them, they quickly brushed me off. But I didn't know how to sell it, or address it, so to speak. When I tried to force the issue, they would shut me down with no explanation. It was the first time I experienced the overt top-down management that I can only imagine you experience in the military. It's the management style that says, "I'm the boss. Do it because I said so. I owe you nothing of an explanation." I went from a boss like Anne Bowman who gave me stock options without even asking, to a boss who wouldn't even have the discussion because I should be "grateful to just have a job." I began to feel like I wasn't valued, even though we were still the winning team and the mission was great. My feelings were compounded by the fact that I was homesick and lonely.

Another top sales leader—a posh, eccentric British man— hated the casual way I dressed. Rackspace had no real dress code. We didn't care what you looked like; we cared about merit. This sales leader wanted everybody to be clean-shaven, and he thought it completely uncouth and disrespectful to wear hats in the office. I was a goatee-bearded, beanie-wearing dude from the US, and he didn't like that at all.

This was one of the few times in my career where I didn't handle myself well. This sales leader felt like my dress code was disrespectful and I felt like Rackspace had allowed this one leader to change the rules on me. If I had been work-ing in sales, I would have understood because it was part of their subculture. But I was in customer support and in customer support we always dressed for comfort. Because of that, we did not hide the fact that we hated each other. It was out in the open. One day he made a comment in passing about my dress code, and I said, "You wanna know why I wear this beanie? Because I can."

For all you out there reading this, I want you to know two

lessons here. First, if you hire the wrong leader, they will introduce conflicting values to the organization and destroy your culture faster than anything else. Second, if you are not professionally mature, you will become part of that problem, which is exactly what I did. I should have used the core values to plead my case and show him why his new fabricated value was not in alignment with the company's values. Instead, I became disgruntled and combative and I am ashamed to admit it,, but it's true. Lucky for me, they fired him before his poison went too far.

But until they did, I was not in a good place.

On an ongoing basis, employees were asked to complete a happy check survey that came straight from Gallup, the same organization that developed CliftonStrengths. It asked ten questions, such as, Do you have a best friend at work? Do you have the tools to do your job? They were thoughtful questions that helped measure, among other things, your satisfaction at work.

When I answered the survey question about having a best friend at work, I answered no. At a time when I needed community and leaders to feel like they cared about me and that I was a valued member, I was instead wounded. One of the top leaders of EMEA walked up to me with their direct report to my desk and jokingly said, "According to this data, you're the most unhappy person in the UK." The survey was supposed to be anonymous. I felt betrayed, and their behavior was a clear violation of our core value of *treating Rackers like friends and family*. Perhaps they thought they were living the *full disclosure* value.

"Is that from the completely anonymous survey I filled out?" I may have thrown in a couple of F-bombs too, and they quickly ran away with their tail between their legs. They realized what they had done, but they never followed up with it. With one careless comment, this leader managed to take away my valued member status in one instant. That's how fast it happens.

ROGUE SUBCULTURES

Team culture or remote culture runs the risk of countering organization culture. If you do not have a strong foundation, this is where your culture can start to unravel. If your leaders don't set the tone, if your mission is BS, if your core values are BS and your leaders don't live them out, then it's fair game at the team level. Hire the wrong leader, and they will compound this issue, hijacking your culture by introducing their own core values that throw people into a state of confusion. The core values and mission are what you can use to prevent rogue subcultures from forming and jeopardizing the overall mission.

For example, Rackspace had strong core values, but oftentimes whenever there was a dispute, someone would use *fanatical support* to get you to do what they wanted or use it to tell you why you're wrong, saying something like, "That's not very fanatical of you." And if you could give a rebuttal that was better than the core value, they would accept it. For example, you might respond that you are short-staffed and had too much work and say, "It's not very friends and family to add a last-minute rush job to a customer service guy who already has a thousand other customer issues that he can't get to. You need to get him some help."

After the CEO and leadership team, managers are the number-one carriers of your culture, and if you have managers going rogue or misusing your core values, they will start the systemic dismantling of your culture.

But just like the US, the EMEA office was growing fast, and growth always brings its own set of troubles.

I knew my time in the EMEA office would be limited, and I kept my eyes open for the best opportunity to return to the US. Early on in my sojourn, Shannon came to London to build stronger relationships with her UK counterparts. After briefly catching up, she could immediately sense that I was not doing well and told me, "Whenever you want to come back to the US, I have a job for you and would love to have you on my team." I will forever be grateful for Shannon, who, from the first time I met her, saw my potential. When

I was ready, she moved heaven and earth to get me back as soon as possible to a great job with a fair salary. I left the UK loving all my peers but feeling very wounded by some of my experiences. Shannon re-engaged me and got me back to my old self.

KEY TAKEAWAYS

- When hiring for diversity, look for diversity of ideas and thought patterns, not just gender and ethnicity.
- Look for actions that you can take to demonstrate to your employees that they are valued members of your winning team by allowing them to show their diversity.
- Find ways to instill your core values in locations beyond your headquarters.

Chapter 4

Making Social Contracts

By the end of my tenure in London, I was in desperate need of personal, organizational, and cultural recovery. I still loved the mission of Rackspace. The London team was a winning team within a winning company, but my enthusiasm and engagement were the lowest they'd ever been. I was one of the highest performers at what I did, but my feedback was not taken seriously. At twenty-five years old, I did not know how to handle being undervalued.

The London management wanted to just tell me what to do, but I was used to a different social contract, one in which you don't tell me what to do without explaining it to me. I had seen the way it was supposed to be (at Rackspace anyway), and this was not the way we worked. In the US environment, I thrived, I was one of the greatest versions of myself there is. But I wasn't thriving in London because the social contract had been changed on me, and I felt abandoned and betrayed.

Lanham used to get onstage at open book meetings and say, "Q&A time. Who's got a Scud missile for me?" He said that because he was asking for the controversial stuff. I was used to asking challenging questions, but I was never disrespectful. I felt like we had all earned the right to demand thoughtful explanations. I would express my displeasure, and because I had such a good brand in the US, they wouldn't fire me. Lanham was so good that he even welcomed it. Every so often at open book, he would flat-out call on me from the stage. "Lorenzo, you have any Scud missiles for me?" and I would say something like, "Sure, why are so many good Rackers leaving from XYZ department? What's going on over there?" I really wanted to say, "Why haven't you fired that crappy leader over in XYZ department who is literally chasing away our most valuable talent?" He was always good about not getting rattled and would always give an answer to the question. That was the dance we did. And I appreciated it because it showed that he wasn't hiding from the issues but instead wanted to know them. He wanted the good, the bad, AND the ugly.

My peers in London were some of the best I have ever worked with, but it's not enough to have your peers feel like you are a valued member. That feeling of value must come from the top. And because I lacked that support from the leadership, I used every break and lunchtime to spread my discontent. I was actually a risk to the London office culture. It would be reasonable to include in a social contract that, "We don't gossip with each other here. If you have a problem, you need to take it to the person or your manager."

In the US, if I had a problem, I could go to my manager. She could either tell me why the thing couldn't be fixed or what she was going to do to fix it. That's okay—at least I could get it off my chest. If she took the issue to a leadership meeting and only she and another guy voted for it, and everyone else voted it down, at least I knew someone was fighting on my behalf and cared about my frustrations. It's very hard to run a company without having some type of process for feedback.

The final straw came for me on a fateful Friday. The UK had a tradition where once a month on a Friday they did something called "Dress Up Smart Day." That is UK slang for dressing up nice. What it meant for EMEA Rackers was the dress code for that day was business professional. If you didn't dress up, they would fine you one pound and give it to charity. By this time, I was so frustrated with the leadership that I just came to work like normal.

My manager at the time pulled me into a room and began

to lecture me about my casual attire. I decided I had experienced enough. I felt they were trying to force a type of culture that didn't exist at Rackspace. I was performing at the highest level, my coworkers loved me, my customers loved me, and mandating that I wear a suit had nothing to do with our core values. I got into a yelling match with her and unloaded all my frustrations. I didn't **treat her like friends and family** that day as I unloaded two years of pent-up pain and anger. I wouldn't leave the UK for a couple of weeks, but that was the day I quit the UK office mentally.

On a professional level, the UK was a turbulent time for me. From a life-lessons standpoint, it was a rich and amazing experience. But it was time for me to go home. I met so many great people in London and was grateful for an experience that I know few people get to have, but when the opportunity to return to San Antonio came up, I grabbed it. My triumphant return, however, would be short-lived.

I returned to the US to take on the role of project manager and business analyst. One of my best friends was a guy named Khaled Saffouri, whom I later nicknamed the Lebanese Brad Pitt because of his larger-than-life personality and rugged good looks. He started with me in that group of six on orientation day. Right before I returned to the US, he moved to London to be the new VP of sales, so we had some overlap time together in the UK. I had been working for about six months or so in my new business analyst role and was really enjoying it. Khaled called me one day at five in the morning and said, "We have a huge problem over here. Our sales machine is too good right now. We've sold more accounts than our enterprise account managers can handle. A couple of them have quit and walked out. A couple of new ones have threatened to mutiny and walk out if we don't slow down and stop selling. You need to come to the UK and train the new account managers. You are the one who has to do it. I need you to share the knowledge of what made you great." Hearing that made me feel so incredibly valuable—and was the start of me healing some of my UK culture wounds. It felt like I was about to be given a second chance, and I would return to the London office as a valued member.

I was still half asleep and told Khaled, "Dude, I'm not even in customer support anymore. But if the need is that bad, I am willing to do it if you can get my boss and their boss to approve it." By the time I got into the office that day, Khaled had worked his magic. Because the need was so great and the UK couldn't just stop producing revenue, my boss approved the transfer, and just like that, I was headed back to the UK. Because I was on a winning team back in the US, I felt valued again. They were hosting me and paying for my housing stipend, so it was a clearly different circumstance. I had good mentors at the time and decided to make the most of it.

I was sad that those account managers in the UK had quit,

but I'm incredibly grateful that it accidentally created an opportunity for my redemption. Upon my arrival, I met with the leader of customer support to extend an olive branch. I told them I was there to help and had no intention of undermining them. They knew I was there to help them. They had let the results go unchecked, and it ended in catastrophe with people leaving that had taken care of customers the most.

This is where **treating other like friends and family** comes into play when you are willing to say, "Hey, we're going to get you guys help." If you're solely dedicated to results, the organization instead says, "Shut your mouth and go back to work. You're lucky to have a job." Or "We can find someone else to do your job if you can't."

Every day I sent an update to everyone who had sponsored me from the US and EMEA leadership side, and the entire team I was training. I went over all the tools I'd shown them and what we were going to do the next day. I did this every day for an entire month. The US was so impressed that my former boss, Shannon, said, "That guy needs to be a leader."

One of the great ways for a leader to show an employee they're valued is to recognize their potential. I always marvel that in a moment when I was trying to find my way back to Rackspace, Shannon saw my potential. Before she saw me as a leader, my brand was that of a great account manager, but also the young, funny guy, maybe even the office clown. When so many leaders wouldn't take me seriously, Shannon was the very first person who said, not only is he great, but he is great enough to lead and manage people. He is good enough to coach a team and help our business advance. If you want to have a culture that wins, go find yourself an army of Shannon Foresters.

She called me and said that when I came back, they would make me a team leader in her division. I could have cried I was so happy. I came back to the US with a promotion and a manager I would run through walls for. My redemption was complete. I was finally back.

Your core values guide your hiring, firing, and decision-making, while your social contracts guide all the informal behavior. Social contracts play a supporting role to your core values and sustain your culture with rules of conduct for both parties—organization and employees. Employees should learn those values and behaviors from day one of their time with you.

ROOKIE ORIENTATION

We were six employees the day I went through orientation at Rackspace in 2001. We did a couple hours of training in the conference room. When I moved back to the US in 2006, onboarding had evolved into a full-blown, rookie orientation, a weeklong training that every new employee went through before being put on the job. That week of training was our cultural indoctrination. It was one of the greatest things we did to scale the culture as the company grew and provided an excellent example for other companies to follow.

First, every single new hire was required to attend—and I mean every single one. In any given Rookie O you could see a Linux engineer sitting next to the new CMO (chief marketing officer—we went through a lot of those). Many companies would excuse their C-level leaders from a "cute" rookie orientation, but we did not. I remember once while traveling, I was waiting at the airport baggage claim. I checked my phone and had an email from our president, Lanham. It said, "Lorenzo, please meet our new COO, Mark Roenigk. He just joined the Rack from eBay and after his Rookie O, I want you to meet with him and become his culture mentor." I was shocked, humbled, and scared shitless. And to be very clear, I learned way more from Mark than he learned from me. But that is the beauty of Lanham's leadership. It didn't matter how important you thought you were, no one got to skip Rookie O. That intentional decision came straight from the top, and it set a great tone for our culture; the first thing you did when you joined our company was learn the way we did things.

Second, new hires are a captive audience without urgent

responsibilities, and Rookie O served as the platform to establish good behaviors right from the start. The founders came in and told the story of starting the company. The core values were explained, and Graham Weston gave a training on CliftonStrengths. We even did cool things like have the Rackspace Foundation give a presentation to raise money for their community projects known as Rack Gives Back. Graham kept a standing policy that he would match whatever amount was raised by the foundation. That one week drove home the point that we cared about our people and our culture. It was part hype-machine, part Rackspace ideology training. And it worked—beautifully.

It doesn't matter what industry you are in, when a company is serious about scaling their culture they will inevitably introduce something like Rookie O. When I worked at H-E-B, the largest privately held grocery company in the US, I went through a similar weeklong training before I ever stepped foot inside the grocery store. They even had a real check-out station with groceries and everything. They were so intentional about their culture and so customer-obsessed that twenty-two years later, I still remember that you don't bag the detergent with the perishable items.

A group of Rackspace employees once visited Zappos, the legendary online shoe company that is famous for its culture. Not only did they do employee culture training, but if you came to see their facility as a *visitor*, they would make you sit through an abbreviated version of their culture training before they gave you a tour of their headquarters. The notion of our Rookie O was to get employees fired up; Zappos took culture to the next level by getting customers, potential customers, and visitors fired up about their culture.

If you want to study an organization that takes scaling and culture training seriously, look up Texas A&M University. They have an entire website dedicated to their traditions. Every year, thousands of incoming freshmen participate in the four-day Fish Camp orientation to learn about the culture and traditions of the university before starting classes. It's a spectacular site to behold when you realize how in sync their fifty-thousand-plus student body is. And as my old sales manager Andrew Gibbens used to say, "They are all singing from the same hymn sheet."

DEFINE YOUR SOCIAL CONTRACTS

According to Dan Ariely's book *Predictably Irrational*, we live in two worlds. One is the world of market contracts where I pay you for something, and I get something in exchange. The other world makes exchanges based on social contracts. We always volunteer more than what the market rate would have been. Ariely explains the concept with this example: if a friend asks you to help him move, you absolutely cancel your plans. You spend all of a Saturday helping him, and when he tries to pay you, you say, "Don't be ridiculous." That's a social contract, whereas if he busted out ten dollars, it's almost an insult because what you're doing is worth way more than ten dollars. If he was getting your help at a market rate, it would be a much higher price.

But how do we define social contracts for workplace cultures?

Merriam-Webster defines a social contract as "an actual or hypothetical agreement among the members of an organized society." The definition that I prefer is from the Urban Dictionary, which defines a social contract as, "The unwritten, unspoken rules of polite society."

Your company's core values are what allow the employees to make decisions when you're not there. But social contracts are a lot of the things we mistake for core values. The reason this happens is because the two are inextricably linked. The core values of your company are also the foundation of your social contract.

Similar to prison life, there are the official rules of the prison, and then there are the unofficial rules of the prison yard. "Don't go there. Don't talk to so-and-so." The social contract represents the unspoken rules of your team, department, and company.

Your core values guide your hiring, firing, and decision-making, while your social contracts guide all other behavior that lies in the gray areas. Social contracts play a supporting role to your core values and sustain your culture with rules of conduct for both parties—organization and employees. In Rackspace customer support, it was things like, "You respond the same day the customer calls in. Don't be demanding with the engineers." In Rackspace sales, it was things like, "At the end of the month, everyone stays late until we hit our goal." That's all social contract language. The market contract is, "I'm paying you fifty-thousand-dollars to be an account manager and you're going to have a thousand customers."

The *New York Times* published a revealing article on Amazon's high-performing and stressful work culture, "Inside Amazon: Wrestling Big Ideas in a Bruising Workplace,"[4] that stirred up a lot of controversy. If I was going to write a basic social contract for Amazon based solely on the article, it would sound like this: "We're going to do a lot of amazing projects (which is part of what makes us the winning team), but your work-life balance is not our number one priority. We will take as much as you are willing to give us. If you want to give up your kid's birthday party and come in on Saturday and work, we will take it." That's the social contract, and then the market contract is, "In return, we're

---

4   https://www.nytimes.com/2015/08/16/technology/inside-amazon-wrestling-big-ideas-in-a-bruising-workplace.html.

going to pay you well and allow you to work on projects that few people will get to experience workwise." Pundits were outraged at the Amazon article, but in my opinion, I liked that they were explicit about how results-oriented they are. If you read their core values, also known as their Leadership Principles, you will see that innovation and customers are their number one priority, not employee happiness. They clearly state what they do, and if you don't like that, maybe it's not the company for you.

Great leaders intuitively understand how having a clear social contract is a powerful tool to help them achieve their inspiring mission. Elon Musk spoke at the annual Air Force Association Symposium about innovation in 2020.[5] This was the event where all of the Air Force's best and brightest were there to learn from the master of innovation. When the host asked him about the culture of innovation, Elon Musk listed three critical ideas:

He said, "The incentive structure is set up such that

1. Innovation is rewarded.
2. Making mistakes along the way does not come with a big penalty.
3. But failure to try to innovate at all comes with a big penalty. You will be fired."

This beautiful, clear example demonstrates how Elon Musk creates a social contract for innovation at his companies. And the social contract underlies the core values of Tesla, SpaceX, and all of Musk's endeavors.

DON'T MAKE PROMISES YOU CAN'T KEEP

Every company should have an honest conversation about what their social contract is. A lot of companies will create social contracts that turn out to be unhealthy. They make a promise without knowing if they can keep it, such as promising a career path for you, which is dangerous. They can't predict the future of their company. What if they're static and stop growing? Will they create positions just so that someone can say they are advancing in their career?

I feel like Rackspace made a similar mistake in all but promising potential recruits that there was nearly guaranteed career progression. A good social contract would say that when opportunities open up, the company prefers to promote from within and will evaluate its own employees first. But that's not the same thing as a guarantee that employees will have room to advance in the company. That sort of social contract sets both parties up for failure.

The reasoning on the part of the company is that such promises will prevent employees from leaving to go to another fast-growing company. I argue that if your culture is strong enough, you can withstand that. You don't need to create artificial social contracts that are hard to enforce.

As a company grows, the social contract, like your core values, may—and often does—change. These are acceptable and expected changes, but you must communicate those changes to employees. And most important, you must communicate the Why. The online retailer Etsy knows this reality all too well. The *New York Times* article, "Inside The ETSY Revolution,"[6] tells the story of Etsy's culture and how devastated their employees were when the company laid off about eighty people, including their beloved founder and CEO, who was ousted by the board for lackluster growth. Their original social contract sold employees on the ideas of saving the environment and self-expression. After Etsy went public and results slumped, their employees learned the hard lesson that this old social contract was not valid when having to choose between being a B-Corp or giving more value to shareholders.

While people want to feel as if their voice is heard, the social contract doesn't imply the organization is a democracy. Leaders will accept feedback from employees, but at the end of the day, leaders with their reputations on the line have to make the final decisions. In other words, business decisions aren't made with democratic votes.

---

6   https://www.nytimes.com/2017/11/25/business/etsy-josh-silverman.html.

THE UNSPOKEN PRISON YARD RULES

At Rackspace, our social contract included that we were a performance-based company, and pedigree didn't matter. If you kicked butt and did an amazing job, there was no limit to your growth. We're here to get a job done and serve customers. When we were in cross-functional teams, one of the most powerful, unwritten parts of our social contract was that we put the needs of the team above the needs of the individual. The sales guy knows he can't sell a terrible deal that benefits him only because he's literally surrounded by people that will have to eat the crap that he just dished out. They will ostracize him and make his life hell. The prison yard rules say you can't be a self-centered jerk in that environment.

The social contract includes those base things you should do anyway, as a good human being. Everybody says they want integrity, but the social contract of your company is where you tell the employee what your version of integrity is. You have to define it with stories, principles, and phrases that actually explain what the social contract is and what the consequences of breaking it are.

Every company has at least a base level of social contracts, and every team has a subset of its own agreement. At Rackspace, we had no dress code, but, as discussed earlier, the sales department had its own unwritten dress code. The company explicitly said, "We don't have a dress code here."

The unspoken rule, however, was, "If you want to be in sales and succeed, you have to dress for success."

At open book meetings, employees could give direct feedback to the executive staff. Sales, however, stuck to a stricter hierarchy than the rest of the company. You couldn't just approach the VP and blurt out feedback. You had to go through the chain of command. Furthermore, if you rarely or never hit your sales quota, your opinion was not that valuable. The table stakes for contributing ideas and helping the sales department improve was first hitting your quota.

The data center team, because they were a small crew stuck in a building that's constantly fifty degrees with thousands of computers getting calls from offices around the world to schedule server hardware upgrades, had their very own culture. They were the "pirates" of the company; they even hung a pirate flag in the data center to show that you could not boss them around. They were a punk rock organization—no dress code; people had mohawks and piercings. They had the most stressful jobs in the company, but they had each other's backs. If you tried to go over their heads, they would punish you later.

If you are a leader, you need to find out and start to write down what your company's social contracts are. But how do you do that? Start where every good detective movie starts: the word on the street.

CULTURE PILLARS

There are employees in your company who, from a culture perspective, are brighter stars than others. They are the high priests of your culture. They have dedicated their loyalty to you because they believe in your mission as if their life depends on it. And, they are not doing it for the money. If you stop and think about who they are, you probably know who they are. If you don't, ask around because their manager, peers, and team know who they are. Ask, "Who are the people that really live our culture?" They are the people who everyone goes to when they need to vent about what the company is doing. Those are your culture pillars. You need to find them, and you need to do two things once you do.

1. **You need to keep them:** One of the most legendary culture pillars at Rackspace was a guy named Larry Reyes, aka, SugarBear. Larry was such an amazing culture pillar that his full-time job became running and emceeing our Rookie Orientation Program. He was so good at coaching new hires on our culture that departments were desperate and angling to have their five minutes at Rookie O and present what their department did to all the new rookies. He even created an award called the Tear it Up award; at the end of Rookie O week, new hires voted for the best presenter. The speaker with the most votes got the highly coveted Tear It Up Award. Across the building, the entire company could hear SugarBear firing up the new Rookie O graduates on graduation

day. His very presence excited you and made you want to jump up and go high-five a new hire and welcome them to the Rack. Rookie O was never the same after SugarBear left. Silence remained where there was once a celebratory procession. Only a fool would try to fill SugarBear's shoes. Your company has culture pillars who are your version of SugarBear. You need to move heaven and earth to keep them.

2. **You need to listen to them:** While I was working in the London office, managing directors came and went faster than waves on the beach. When the third managing director in as many months was close to being fired, Graham called me. He said the executive staff had some concerns about the leadership in the London office and wanted to know what was going on. Due to the level of trust I had built with Graham in the US when we shared a cubicle, he was accustomed to me giving him the unvarnished truth. I told him the current guy wasn't any better than his predecessor, but that there were two close friends of mine who had a better understanding, and he should call them. Their names were Pravesh Mistry and Darren Norfolk. Graham called them, and they willingly listed all of their concerns about the managing director. Graham asked them to repeat everything they'd just said to our CEO Lanham. They did that, and Lanham said, "Will you do me a favor and say all the concerns that you just told me to the guy himself?" It was a really gutsy move, but they did it like troopers,

then the next day, he was let go. During the ordeal, my friend Pravesh said Graham was so concerned about the company. Once Pravesh had told Graham everything, Graham asked for one more favor. He said, "Please, take care of our customers." And he hung up. His parting words left such an impression on us as young men. Graham never lost sight of what we were there to do, which was to serve our customers. Removing a managing director is like removing a CEO, yet, despite a huge organizational regime change, the customers come first.

Before Rackspace went IPO, the social contract had *fanatical support* as the number one lens and prism through which we looked at our customers. After the IPO, that part of the social contract subtly changed to another number one prism—shareholder value.

For me, the IPO was the beginning of the end.

KEY TAKEAWAYS

- Create social contracts that align and support your core values.
- Communicate your social contracts to employees.
- If your social contract changes, tell your employees so behavior continues to align with beliefs.
- Identify your culture pillars and do all you can to keep them at your company.

Chapter 5

Going Public

In the time leading up to IPO, I was a team leader and managed a Linux team in the enterprise division, and Shannon Forester-Smykay was my manager. She was more worldly, more experienced. There have been a lot of people in my career who saw my potential, but only a few that actually went out of their way to help me achieve it. Shannon went out of her way to make me a leader and a manager, and she did it when no one else would have ever bet on me if their life depended on it.

She also knew what was coming, and she created a culture that insulated me in a good way from the post-IPO shift we were about to experience. The leadership team had separated our enterprise division into three divisions within the main one. Shannon ran one of the three, called Proactive, and it was the least prestigious one that had the customers nobody wanted. Shannon loved it because she was that good. It's one of the main reasons I loved her; she had the underdog spirit, just like me. She brought me and the other two leaders into an office with a spreadsheet of everybody who reported to us and their salaries. She said some of them were grossly underpaid, and she was working to bring them up to their market value. I loved her leadership.

A Linux engineer on my team who used to work at a burger drive-through had his salary bumped up to market rate. When I gave him a Post-It note with his new salary on it, he tried to keep from crying. He asked if he could take the Post-It home and put it on his refrigerator. We had so many stories like that. Shannon was still living our core values and it had a profound effect on how I viewed leadership and people. She was my very first leadership mentor.

It was a difficult time to be giving raises, but down market or not, Shannon could not stand the injustice of what some of our people were getting paid. She was eloquent at pitching her superiors and determined to prioritize her people. We all knew that she was in our corner. We called her Mama Shannon, and she wore that nickname with pride.

Shannon taught me what it meant to be a manager. For example, I had a guy who came in late all the time. I complained about it to her and said I was going to send an email to the whole team. Knowing this was the biggest rookie manager mistake of all time, she pulled me aside. She told me, "Look, you're going to disengage all your best people by doing that. Why send an email to everybody, including the people who show up on time, when you should just pull that guy in directly and talk to him?" She knew I was afraid of the conflict, but she didn't scold me or embarrass me for it. I was a first-time manager and she took her time explaining the Why to me. Everything she taught me made sense; she was always right. I got real coaching from her.

IT TAKES MONEY TO MAKE MONEY

It was explained to me that going public meant taking Rackspace from being a private company to being publicly traded on the New York Stock Exchange. It was one of the many lessons in business that I didn't know anything about but was about to get a crash course in. Graham Weston, when asked about when the right time was to raise money, said, "You only raise money when you have something specific to raise it for. Uber raised billions because they had a very specific reason: to launch in every major city in the world." The main reason to go public is to raise money after you've tapped out your friends and relatives and venture capitalists.

Rackspace needed lots of money. We were growing like crazy and business was good, but the growth rate we were headed toward could not be reached without huge amounts of capital. At our rate of growth, we needed to build new data centers, buy tons of servers, and hire lots of people to support them. While the growth would result in more revenues, implementing the pieces to get there required multiple millions of investment dollars upfront. So, the "why" behind going public made perfect sense to me.

It's what happened after that I really wasn't prepared for.

The buzz around going public was unlike anything I have ever experienced. We all knew it was going to happen but when it would happen and how it would change what we did every day were all unknowns. A lot of employees had shares that would take on a monetary value as soon as Rackspace went public, and there was an underlying tension of who had shares and who didn't.

We were also forbidden to talk about going public with anyone who wasn't a Racker. At one of our open meetings, Lanham explained the concept of insider trading and that we were about to enter something called the "Quiet Period." You couldn't even tell your spouse what was going on and if anything about Rackspace going public leaked, the person who shared the information risked being hauled into court if not off to jail. Even though it was serious and scared me, I still found it a little funny. I imagined being in prison and some tough guy asking what I was in for and saying, "I tweeted we had a good month revenue wise. I'm hardcore like that."

RINGING THE BELL

As a young man whose sole business training up until that time was Rackspace open book meetings, I naively thought this was the finish line for our inspiring mission. It was as if Rackspace was going to reveal the magic of *fanatical support* to the world and they would judge us as worthy or unworthy. It felt like the fanciest, most business-y beauty pageant of all time.

On the actual day of the IPO announcement on the New York Stock Exchange, the executive staff stood on a stage and rang the opening market bell. Back in San Antonio, we all got bells, so while the leadership team was ringing the bell, we at Rackspace rattled our cowbells. Someone made a cool graphic that had Yoda on it and said, "Public we are." I have no doubt everyone felt like a valued member of a winning team on an inspired mission that day.

That was one of the biggest milestones of my career. I wondered, "Will the market, whatever that is, believe in our mission too? Will they see how special we are? Will they see the company I love and love it too?" More importantly, I realized that I had helped make this happen. Every call I took, every customer I saved from churning, every upgrade—all of it had, in some small way, helped push our company to this goal. I am still proud of that contribution to this very day.

We did not know that August 2008 was also the beginning

of the worst recession in a long time. We opened at $12.50 and fell to $10. It broke a lot of people's hearts, but it didn't break my heart. Since the shares I owned were given to me, it was all upside—for me, Rackspace shares were like lottery tickets and I had a winning ticket.

I felt the disappointment most of us had when trading closed that day and wanted to fight the market that had undervalued us, wanting to show them who we were. And I would fight it by going back to my desk and serving our customers.

SCALING WITH EXPERIENCE

There had been an attempt to go public once before. Our inevitable fate was to be acquired or go public—that was always going to be the outcome. Normal employees were shielded from those situations because all we ever talked about was *fanatical support* and serving our customers, which was part of our success. Ironically, to get to the next stage of IPO, growing and scaling, we had to lose what had actually enabled us to reach that point.

One of the principles that I have observed over the years, but first learned at Rackspace during that time is this:

Rapid growth exposes all of your weaknesses.

The time frame between the different generations of

Rackspace leadership was relatively short. At the time, Rackspace had a successful IPO, generation two leadership began to slowly wind down. The company was founded in 1998 by three Trinity University students; Richard Yoo, Patrick Condon, and Dirk Elmendorf. In 2001 when I started, they had already realized they'd need partners to help run and scale the business. It took a lot of humility and non-ego for the founders to step aside. They graciously became figureheads, not trying to prove they were the smartest guys in the room.

They brought in Graham, Morris, Lanham, and Lew Moorman as generation two leadership. Their era lasted until around the end of 2013 and was the most formidable time period during which Rackspace was brought to its dominance. During that run, Rackspace hired more than a hundred people a month for almost ten years straight.

When you grow fast, you see the gaps and broken processes in everything you do from hiring people and onboarding to automating tasks and production. At Rackspace, we were growing fast, and one of our biggest problems was how to scale the business to keep up with our growth and demand. Going public would help us scale the company. Going public also meant that we needed to go out and hire people who could help us take the business from running things with duct tape and string to real systems and processes that were reliable and repeatable.

Much like the way Glenn Reinus came in to scale and bring order, process, and bring a system to sales, the IPO would allow Rackspace to hire high-caliber people to scale the other parts of the business—an army of Glenn's coming in to help us, only in all departments and divisions of the company. I imagined someone like him coming to customer support and teaching us the ways of large-scale corporations. And I was excited about learning from them.

We hired some amazing people. People like Mark Roenigk, who came from eBay, had the swagger of John Wayne, and made me up my operation game. People like John Lionato from GE, who taught me Lean Six Sigma and gave me tools that I absolutely still use today.

IPO gave me personally tools, resources, and connections that I carry with me to this day. But like every good thing in life, there is also the underbelly.

PEDIGREE OVER PERFORMANCE

As the IPO date approached in 2008, Rackspace began bringing in leaders who would become generation three and started making seismic changes to the culture. I commend what our executive team was doing as they wanted to bring in people who could scale the business and get it where it needed to go. Lanham was a pedigree-over-performance guy; it was inherent in his nature. I assume it was because he held a Harvard MBA, but I am not sure. What I am sure of is that lots of new faces started showing up with fancy resumes.

Post-IPO Rackspace immediately changed the hiring practices. They wanted people with MBAs and Ivy League degrees who had worked for big company names like EDS, HP, and Dell. The intentions were good; they needed to appeal to the shareholders and sound good in press releases. But in my opinion, that's when a lot of the core values and culture were sacrificed in order to get the people who could help us scale.

On one hand, it was good because some of these new pedigreed people added immediate value and introduced processes and systems that we desperately needed. On the other hand, I would wager that the vast majority of them did not. There is no doubt in my mind that we allowed so many bad hires in, knowing they did not share our core values purely because their resume had a big company logo on it. And what was so off-putting to me was that so many of them had an air of superiority and snobbery that I wasn't used to seeing at Rack. To me, it ran counter to our value of *treating others like friends and family*. And even more frustrating for me was that I thought so many of them weren't bringing any of the value that their fancy resume alluded to, yet they were treated so special. I was soured by the situation, and my frustrations seemed to grow with every new big company hire.

While I was a team leader in Intensive, everyone in leadership was super-excited about a new sales guy we had just hired from Harvard. He was supposed to be the next big thing and was being fast-tracked to leadership, no doubt. I rolled my eyes. The pedigree over performance was so counter to our *results first* core value that I found myself secretly rooting against the guy. I wanted him to fail. And sure enough, when the quotas came due, this Harvard boy couldn't sell his way out of a paper bag. I remember talking to a couple of other old-school Rackers, and we all felt the same way. None of us wanted him to succeed. I am ashamed to say this, but I was happy when he finally left as a failure. Why? Because Rackspace had given us a social contract that told us that results and performance would dictate the trajectory of our progression. When we saw how they treated guys like this, we knew the social contract had been broken, and we felt betrayed.

DON'T FORGET TO LOOK INSIDE

David Bryce once told me, "When you start a company, you have to hire from the outside. But once a company has a pool of people, it's important to promote from within as much as possible." Like all things in life, there has to be balance. Glenn was masterful at promoting from within but hiring from outside the company when he needed a skill that no one on the team possessed.

Within customer support, two of our greatest leaders came from the most unexpected places. Sally Aguilar Robertson started at Rackspace as a billing specialist, and Marcus Robertson was an overnight windows engineer. Had David Bryce not seen their potential, I bet no one would have ever given them a shot. They would both go on to be two of the most beloved and influential leaders in our company. They also got married.

It's easy to overlook the people who are already there. It's also easy to underpay them because most of the time, they were the early employees to sign on and take a chance on your crazy company. But consider this: leaders like Sally and Marcus were exceptional at their jobs, and it was easy for anyone to see that they already got the core values and lived them out.

David said, "When you take someone who has worked their way up, has been a success at everything, has relationships with everyone, and you promote them, it sends a message to everyone that they could do it too." I remember the day I got promoted to senior manager, a guy came up to me and said, "It's so nice to see one of the good guys get promoted for once."

There will no doubt be a real need to bring on people from the outside, and that is totally ok, but don't forget the crew you have.

THE REBRAND OF OLD RACKERS

Throughout my career, I've been coached and trained by people who are curious by nature and always ask probing questions. *Tell me more* and *Why* are two of the greatest tools in their toolbox. They were critical thinkers who were taught to ask for clarity and that's a principle I've lived by. My number two strength in Clifton is "restorative," which is problem-solving.

One of the oldest conflicts that I have had to face in my career is asking why when a big change is proposed. I don't ask this question to be obstinate or negative. I loved the ***embrace change for excellence*** core value. I simply asked it so I can understand where the change is coming from. It comes from a place of problem-solving and context. A leader who has a big ego will say, "Because I said so. Do it because I'm the boss, and I told you to." That's never worked for me. A good leader will explain it and coach you through it.

When the new hired guns entered the company, there were a lot of old-school Rackers who immediately got into skirmishes with these new corporate johnnies. The hired guns, pulling out a tactic that I am sure they learned at other big companies, did something unexpected. When they realized that the old-school Rackers were free-thinkers and were not afraid to push back, they rebranded us. It was a genius move with devastating effects.

In the past, being a Racker of tenure carried prestige and honor. Having a low badge number meant we had worked and toughed out through some low points. We got the culture because we had lived and even thrived in it enough to last this long. Many had been promoted along the way.

When the hired guns got pushback from old-school Rackers, they would go into a leadership meeting and say the following:

> *"These old-school Rackers are very difficult. None of them like change. They all want to keep doing things the old way."*

And just like that, we were rebranded.

In a few short months, being an old-school Racker went from being something awesome to a disadvantage. For the first time in my Rackspace life, I hid the fact that I was one of them.

Long-time Rackers began being pushed out, and soon big company people set their sights on Shannon. She moved to another department before they could push her out. Knowing I was good friends with her, the big company guys pulled me aside and asked if I was on their team or not. I found their tactic interesting and thought to myself, "You must think I'm an idiot. I've watched all the prison movies. I know how this ends if I don't say what you want to hear."

So, I politely smiled, nodded my head, and said, "Yes, I'm on your team."

But the new company guys started to see a problem with unhappy people and people jumping to other departments. They called me in and said, "Lorenzo, we noticed that you never bother us with your customers. You just take care of business. When you bring problems to us, you already have solutions. We want to promote you to be a senior manager with two teams here and one team in Austin." I was honored and I thanked them. They promoted another woman on the same day, and I realized we were two of the longest-tenured people in our division. I felt cheapened by my promotion. I knew they were taking heat for pushing out Mama Shannon and other old-school leaders, and they were trying to show that they valued the old-timers with these two quick promotions. Shortly after that, they hired one of their buddies, who reported to me. I had access to the salary numbers for everyone who reported to me, and I saw that the new guy made sixty-thousand-dollars more than me. They were fast-tracking him. During that time, I felt like social contracts were getting ripped up left and right across the company.

I looked around and wondered why these people were brought in. I looked at our CEO Lanham and thought that if I were him, I'd want the board to let me pick my own team. I was also conflicted because I disagreed with what he was doing, but ultimately it was his decision. Graham was as much a figurehead as the founders. Because he was so approachable, a lot of people were pushing back, saying the culture was changing and it wasn't good. The line of old Rackers scheduling time to plead their case to him was getting longer and longer. Like a good parent, he listened and genuinely tried to help as best he could. But in the end, he had to let all these new leaders swing under the protection of Sovereignty of the Boss, which I will explain shortly.

Seeing the people I loved getting hurt, like Shannon and other old-timers, angered me. If I remove myself and look at it from an outside perspective, I realize they had to at least try the avenue of hiring experienced people from big companies. It was the logical play. Our generation two leadership was just trying to figure out how to do it. At some point, they had to say, "We're growing so fast that, if the new VP is going to push out an old Racker, I have to let it play out because I can't get involved in every skirmish."

INVESTORS CHANGE THE SOCIAL CONTRACT

I underestimated the dark side of IPO and the changes it would bring. When a company accepts funding, especially from a venture capital firm, a financial social contract supersedes all others:

"At some point, we want our money back plus a profit. At some point, you will grow so big that we will go public and get our money back, or you will sell the company and get our money back, or you will go out of business. We are ok with you building an amazing culture as long as it incentivizes your employees to grow the company to get us our return."

When a company takes an investment, the social contract includes this clause, whether you like it or not.

The clause changes slightly if the company has gone public:

"There is a new stakeholder who now holds the most power in our social contract. That stakeholder is known as the *Shareholder*. Everything you do, including all the awesome perks of your culture, should be in service of creating and increasing shareholder value. If you do not do this, you better have a powerful reason why and be willing to tell us when you will be back on the shareholder value road. Otherwise, the board will send someone in who will do this."

I did not understand this principle when Rackspace went public. If I had known it, my expectations would have been a lot different, although the change probably still would have hurt like hell.

I'm not a cynic, but I am a realist. In the age of Silicon Valley unicorns, where employees are wooed and lured by stories of amazing culture, you absolutely must evaluate the financial social contract of your company. Of course, there are unicorn exceptions to this rule: when Amazon purchased Zappos in 2009, part of the negotiation was that Zappos run independently, which gave their leadership the flexibility to keep their culture intact.

Patagonia has remained a private company since it opened its doors in 1973. For the most part, they are able to chart their own culture course. They have the freedom to do radical things that most investors or shareholders would not stand for—such as investing heavily in the environment, which does not help increase their bottom line.

Most people who want to work for a great company put culture on their list of job criteria. If you don't, then when the contract is broken or changed, you are going to feel betrayed. So, choose wisely.

BUSINESS LESSON: YOUR CULTURE WILL CHANGE

Outside funding and going public will change your culture. There—the ugly truth is out. When a company answers to shareholders, the prime directive becomes *return on investment* and that directive will influence your culture, perhaps more than any other change that IPO brings.

This means that whoever funded you is ok with the soda machine, the yoga classes, the mindfulness nap rooms, as long as the results are there. But in the absence of growth, profit, and momentum, the people who funded you will cut those things out of your company without batting an eyelash.

A MANAGER VS. A COACH

If culture is like the immune system for a business, then managers are the white blood cells. When they are functioning properly, they protect the business from infectious disease, which in this case, are people that are a bad fit. The problem is that becoming a manager is the most well-known and fastest way in the business world to acquire two things:

1. Power/Influence
2. More money

These are not bad desires in and of themselves. But they are bad reasons to become a manager. I have come to believe over the years that the best managers are more like coaches than anything else. Any company that wants to keep its culture strong, healthy, and thriving needs to have a very intentional strategy to turn its managers into coaches. Of all the tactics I described in this book, this one part of your business has the most leverage in terms of your culture at scale. If you want to get a real pulse for how healthy or unhealthy your culture is right now, go investigate the middle management layer. You will be able to tell very quickly who is just a manager and who is a coach.

In basketball, the coach is always someone who has played the game, so when they give you direction, they know what they are talking about. I have seen so many bad managers who have never done the job of their direct reports. They sit far off, looking down from the ivory tower to make sure their minions get the job done. They avoid getting dirty at all costs. In our world, it was like pulling teeth to get a bad manager to actually get on the phone and talk to a customer. Yuck.

A good coach knows how and when to rally the troops. At Rackspace, our sales team was famously good at this. End-of-the-month time came, and the sales leaders were out there working the troops into a frenzy. They would get on the phone and close deals with their reps. The exceptional ones also knew how the individuals needed to be motivated and didn't treat them all the same.

My buddy Khaled Saffouri was a legendary sales leader and if you passed by his desk on any given day, you would find two stacks next to his laptop. One stack was Starbucks gift cards, and the other was a stack of stationery for hand-written notes.

Like the five love languages,[7] a good coach knows which teammate needs a word of affirmation and who needs a gift to incentivize their effort. A bad manager doesn't care about any of this stuff and just likes to bark orders. They are the generals and everyone else is the soldiers who need to do their bidding.

---

7   Gary Chapman, *The Five Love Languages: The Secret to Love that Lasts*, Northfield Publishing (2014).

The final insight that a good coach has is knowing each team members' strengths and weaknesses. This allows them to evaluate each situation and make a decision based on the team's skills. It helps the leader know when to substitute the right team player in at the right time.

In hindsight, Rackspace was developing a thick layer of upper-middle management, which caused problems because they weren't an army of leaders who wanted to be coaches. They were an army of people who wanted to build their own kingdom, and that's when culture starts to descend.

You also have situations where the company wants to recruit a high-flyer but doesn't have a role for them, so they create a new position. At one point, they said they were going to create a senior manager role, a senior director role, and a senior VP. Post-IPO, we had over two hundred people who were given a director title, and there were only sixty people reporting to them. How can you have over a hundred people with director titles that have no one reporting to them? Middle management syndrome. This increasing layer of middle management is where all the warring, politicking, kingdom-building, and stock-grabbing happened. That layer became poisonous to what we were doing.

EMBRACING CHANGE TO BUILD KINGDOMS

One of the core values, *embracing change for excellence*, opened the way for a lot of the kingdom-building. The big company guys began to slowly dismantle the cross-functional teams that we had implemented so long ago. I'm sure it started with some double vice president of finance that we recruited from Yahoo looked at our teams and saying, "If I can pull all those billing people out of those cross-functional teams and have a team of a hundred people reporting to me, then it makes it easier for me to go back to Lanham and say, "Look at my organization. I should be compensated with a lot more stock." Or if I'm the intergalactic vice president of security from Cisco and want all of the security guys working with me, I will use fancy security terms like Sarbanes-Oxley to justify my flimsy case. Meanwhile, the customer doesn't give a crap about any of that stuff. The reason sounded good on paper, but it was nothing more than kingdom-building. Their kingdoms got bigger and bigger, and the customer experience got worse and worse. The creation of department silos ushered in the dawn of us against them, resulting in internal conflicts and turf wars.

Also, the higher-ups from big companies usually aren't used to getting dirty. They like having the infrastructure so they don't personally deal with customers or employees. They have others to do that. After I left Rackspace, there was a marketing VP who did not allow anyone to talk to him directly. You had to go through one of his other people. Rackspace had given me so much and I loved the company, but watching these people come in angered me. I felt like they were raiding the cupboards, and some of them didn't even last long. They would get into turf wars and leave, but not without filling their portfolio with Rackspace stock first.

SOVEREIGNTY OF THE BOSS

My new director understood that old Rackers were being rebranded and felt bad about it. He went out of his way to treat me with the utmost respect. I was feeling the politics happening. At the open book meeting, I started hearing things that raised red flags. Previously leaders would say they wanted to build something good enough for us to retire there. Immediately after IPO, someone from the leadership team said, "Everybody's got a last day at Rackspace." That language had never been used before. We used to talk about *fanatical support*, and now we talked about shareholder value, which didn't compute.

This is when I believe Rackspace started diverging from our mission and core values. I went to Graham and said I didn't like my boss, who, in turn, didn't like making decisions. When the other two leaders and I went to our boss with issues, he would turn the question around and ask us what we should do. Small or large, the issue size didn't matter. He always asked us what we should do. I didn't need to learn the Socratic method of thinking, I needed leadership and guidance. I neither respected him nor thought he knew what he was doing. He never offered an answer but simply asked what we should do and moved on with his day. Not once did he sell us on his vision, and as a leader, he was uninspiring, to say the least.

In my bitch session with Graham, I desperately and naively wanted him to just fire the guy, but I would soon realize I was barking up the wrong tree. Graham said to me, "Lorenzo, I have this philosophy called *sovereignty of the boss*, which says that when we hire a leader, that leader deserves the autonomy to pick their own teams, make their own rules, and run the business the best way they see fit until such time as they violate our core values and we have to fire them." It was the most beautifully articulate, gracious way of putting the smackdown on me. It made perfect sense to me. Grudgingly, I knew that if someone I managed complained about me, I would want Rackspace leadership to let me try it my way first. I went back and tried to make do the best way I could. I believe that sovereignty of the boss is an essential part of your social contract with leaders.

Middle Management Syndrome is the grand challenge of company culture. If your company has a toxic culture, I am willing to bet you right now that a large part of it is your middle management layer. Sadly, no one has figured this out and this is literally the curing of cancer for company cultures. You can figure out hiring and scaling, but how do you keep the middle-management layer honest? That is the grand challenge that must be solved.

WEALTH CREATION

The distribution of stock and the disparity of salaries between old-time Rackers and the hired guns brought out the worst in most of us. "Unfair" took on a new meaning for me.

The notion that "fairness is primal" comes from the book *The Power of 2: How to Make the Most of Your Partnerships at Work and in Life.* It tells the story of capuchin monkeys who were trained to trade currency. They gave the capuchin a cucumber if the capuchin would trade them for a pebble. Once they taught him currency exchange, they put two capuchin monkeys in abutting cages so they could see each other. They went to the first capuchin and gave him a cucumber for a pebble. They went to the second monkey and gave him a grape for the same pebble. Apparently, capuchins love grapes more than cucumbers. The first one sees it and freaks out. He throws the cucumber back, throws a fit, and refuses to play next time.

Going public creates an incredible amount of wealth for those involved, from company leadership and early employees with stock options to venture capital investors.

I believe most companies that go public genuinely want to do the right thing and make sure that this new wealth is distributed evenly and fairly.

But managing wealth creation is a tricky business, and dare I say a dangerous one. Companies can learn from the Rackspace story, and the best way to handle this complicated issue is to have some rules and principles. So, here is the good, the bad, and the ugly of wealth creation.

CHANGED LIVES AND COMMUNITIES

There are several types of ways to get company stock. The stock I held was literally given to me by my boss Anne Bowman. For me, it was free money if the stock did well. I could argue that I earned it, but at the end of the day, I'd received a winning lottery ticket and I am so grateful—that stock changed my financial destiny, allowed me to pay off debt, and enabled me to write this book.

However, I would not advise anyone reading this book to follow my story as a wealth-creation strategy.

I later learned that there were several people who raised or borrowed huge sums of money to buy more stock options. In the end, these people made great fortunes, but their bet was very different from mine. I wouldn't lose anything if Rackspace failed. These men and women bet the farm that we would succeed, but had it failed, they would have faced financial ruin. Their funding helped Rackspace grow and I am thankful that they made all their money back and then some. At the same time, someone who puts their savings on the line will make decisions to at least preserve, and at best, grow that investment. They're motivated to protect their investment, not necessarily the culture of the company.

Rackspace also had a stock option plan that automatically gave people shares. If you stuck around long enough for them to vest, you got a bonus that fell somewhere between small and paying off your car. There were a lot of people who received enough stock options to do things like pay off student loans, their mortgage, or start that small business they always wanted.

In the final analysis, the wealth created from Rackspace changed many people's lives, mine included. It also changed the city of San Antonio.

When Dell went public in Austin many years before we did, it created so many millionaires that they were nicknamed the Dellionaires. These Dellionaires were the financial capital foundation for what would become the Austin startup and tech scene. On a much smaller level, the wealth generated from Rackspace had a similar effect on San Antonio, the city was forever changed because of this one company.

Many people who were granted stock options said a polite "thank you" and got back to work. Other people were more direct in asking for stock, lobbying, and politicking for more stock options, and this is where it gets tricky.

THE 80/20 SPLIT

During open book, Graham and Lanham often mentioned the Pareto Principle or the 80/20 Rule. As I explained earlier, historically, twenty percent of the customers accounted for eighty percent of the revenue.

Post-IPO, the 80/20 rule showed up in an unseemly fashion. When a company goes public, all stock distributions must be filed with the SEC and it becomes public knowledge. I can go online and look up people, past and present, who have worked at Rackspace and see how much stock they were given. If you took out the investors, the people that personally had raised money to buy more, and the leadership team, it was very hard to look at the way stock was handed out throughout the company. It was even harder to see bad leaders who were terrible fits cause a lot of disruption then leave with more stock than most of the employees would ever get. Just before we went public, I learned of a recent hire renegotiating his stock options in light of the pending IPO. It all just seemed unfair to me—especially because I knew if I tried the same thing, HR would have told me to go back to my desk and get back to work.

What's more, the distribution was uneven among average employees; stock was not allocated in proportion to the amount of work that was done. The 20 percent that did 80 percent of the work were not given the commensurate financial benefit. It is common in companies that the early employees aren't necessarily the best employees, but they have predominance because of seniority. But should it be seniority? Or should it be the 80/20 principle? I argue that with the *results first* core value, if the 80/20 principle is true, then who are the 20 percent of employees who are getting results? They should be the ones rewarded. It shouldn't matter if you're the veteran on the basketball team. If you're not making baskets, they're going to bench you or trade you.

But those who got the stock were not the same 20 percent doing the work. In fact, a lot of the contributing 20 percent didn't get anything at all while many who were outside of that 20 percent, who were good at politics were getting huge chunks. Many people were angrier than a monkey who'd been given a cucumber.

THE TRUE NATURE PRINCIPLE

The wealth distribution of Rackspace is still very hard for me to reconcile because money is such a complicated and emotional topic. There is a good reason the Good Book says, "Where your treasure is, there your heart will be also."

I had, and still have, so many mixed feelings about the subject. I am grateful for what they gave me when they really didn't have to give me anything. I am bummed that so many people who—in my mind—deserved stock didn't get any, or what they did receive didn't match the value they added. I was disappointed and angry to see so many unworthy people profit far more than their contribution to the company; the way they treated people was the opposite of ***treating others like friends and family***. But of all these conflicting feelings, there is one absolute principle that I learned through the Rackspace stock distribution:

When someone stands to gain a lot of money or lose a lot of money, his or her true nature will emerge instantly.

If someone has it inside them to stab you in the back and lie to your face to get a lot of money or avoid losing a lot of money, they will absolutely do it as fast as you can blink. If someone is generous and has a generous heart, even when they risk losing a lot of money, you will also see that generosity come out. The potential of wealth reveals this in a person faster than any other circumstance. And that is the biggest lesson I learned from our IPO.

POLITICS HAPPEN EVERYWHERE

In the early days, our strategy was to deliver *fanatical support* to as many people as we could. After the IPO, people spent lots of time thinking about different things, such as, "What meetings do I need to be seen attending?" One post-IPO manager told a friend of mine that she only had her one-on-one employee meetings out in the open at a very specific table next to the C-suite offices. She intentionally wanted them to see her when they passed by so her profile would be raised.

Although I knew they existed, I'd never gotten all that involved in office politics, and I couldn't believe someone could spend their time strategizing like that. It felt as if there were more people strategizing their careers than people trying to strategize our company mission.

Every company has politics. It is not a reasonable assertion to say you're not going to have politics. If you have a lemonade stand and you hire one person, you're going to have politics, just at varying degrees. Things can be done to limit the politics, which is why we have core values and social contracts.

The politics get larger as the company grows, and politics will lead to toxic behavior, miscommunication, gossip, and fear. When you're a fast-growing company, your bad hires do more damage. They infect your company faster, and it takes ten times longer to fix them. Having one bad leader when you're a small company stands out; having a bad leader during the IPO that affects a three hundred-person division of your company can be catastrophic. Even if you take that guy out of the mix, he has already set the tone for all of his managers to operate the way he was. When you get to a certain level of a company, the poison affects way more people and the antidote takes even longer to cure. With the IPO and the big company hires, Rackspace handed huge portions of the business to people who were not in alignment with the culture, so all kinds of disruptions happened on all fronts. Ongoing growth and profit obscured the changes.

The reality of hiring is that you're going to inevitably hire bad people. Removing those bad hires must be one of your top priorities as a company if you want to maintain your culture as you grow. I know it sounds cliché, but the old saying is very true, "Hire slow, fire fast." If you allow bad leaders to stay too long, you are indirectly encouraging and promoting their bad behavior. You cannot escape these consequences, which is why I want to show you the value of core values, a strong mission, and great social contracts. These are the only ways for your culture, which is your immune system, to defend itself when the inevitable attacks come.

EMPLOYEE AGAINST LEADER

My friend Dax was working for a new division in sales, crushing it. He'd been recruited by an awesome mentor. One of the up-and-coming corporate guys wanted that division, and I saw Dax's mentor and the big company guy politically duke it out. The corporate guy won, and Dax's mentor quit before he was fired. Once Dax started working for the corporate guy, a former Marine, he told me, "They're absorbing us." I told him, "You are going to have to literally move into a new role. You will have to go from sales to customer service, leave your profession or leave the company because the guy who just out-politicked your mentor does not like guys like us. If he tells us to do something and we ask why, he will say he doesn't have to tell us why. He was a Marine and if his general told him to charge a hill, he charged it with no questions asked."

That was the beginning of the "us versus them" mentality, the power plays. Suddenly there were power dynamics where before it was about collaboration. Old-time Rackers couldn't just stop asking questions and voicing concerns because for eight years, that's what we had been trained to do.

Sure enough, Dax asked questions. The Marine told him to get on board and stop pushing back, and Dax quit and went to a competitor. He no longer felt like a valued part of a winning team, and how can you stay in love with a mission that allows that to happen? It broke my heart that my best friend left because of a political skirmish that had nothing to do with him.

Dax was one of the very first old-school culture pillars to leave the company, and, because it was such a new occurrence, our leadership did not know how to handle it. When someone like Dax leaves, it feels like a break-up, and they took it very personally. The day he put in his two weeks, they were about to have security escort him out, but Dax calmly convinced them to let him say his goodbyes and then let that be his last day. This first instinct to lash out would be a foreshadow of what was to become the norm, sadly.

INSPIRING MISSION VS. SHAREHOLDER VALUE

When I did exit interviews, people commonly complained they were dissatisfied with the strategies their leaders implemented that were so off of our inspiring mission. For example, we were a service company that was servicing something very technical, but I found that post-IPO, a lot of brilliant people didn't want to tell their family at Thanksgiving that they worked for a service company. They wanted to say they worked for a tech company, so the big company guys tried to adjust our mission to be technology-focused.

A wavering mission contributed to going off track. Someone might say, "We need to start doing machine learning." The correct answer should be, "I think machine learning is awesome. How does that help us deliver *fanatical support* to our customers?" Instead of asking that question, though, post-IPO leadership would push these ideas as company strategy. Then, it was as if we needed to be in the "next hot tech thing" versus the mission to be one of the world's greatest service companies. There's nothing about technology in that mission statement. That doesn't mean we can't have tech, but when you stop enforcing the mission and stop comparing things to it, you've declared a free-for-all, and that's dangerous in a company. That should only be done at the highest levels of a company.

We were now in a world where pockets of great culture, where people still cared about *fanatical support*, were getting smaller every day. The company was still a winning team, but I didn't feel like I was on a winning team within that team. I wanted my team to respect me and have my back. Seeing the kind of people who were brought in, the money they were paid, the decisions they made, the language they used, I began to ask myself, "Is our mission real, or is it bullshit?" And I started thinking about my own exit.

KEY TAKEAWAYS

- As you prepare for IPO, write down the structure and rules for employee stock options.
- Employees who've been with you from the beginning hold the keys to your core values and culture; recognize and reward their value.
- As you scale and hire experienced, pedigreed employees, make sure they align with your core values.

Chapter 6

The Last Core Value

Authors Kelley Freeman and Rick Jernigan wrote a book called *C.O.A.C.H.*, and although I have never read the book, I love their subtitle, which is *The Final Act of Leading is Leaving*. When people I admired and respected starting leaving Rackspace, I realized the statement, "Everyone has a last day at Rackspace," was true. It's what happens after someone makes the decision to leave that I didn't realize matters as much as everything else.

I believe there is a core value that every single company has that no one ever talks about. It's a core value that I have seen done so terribly over and again at so many companies. It is the act of leaving a company and how you treat someone when they leave. So many people don't think of this as a core value but rather something that managers and human resources handle. But they are absolutely wrong. The way you act when someone resigns or gets fired sends as much of a signal to the entire company as your most cherished traditions. I would say it sends a stronger message.

If you treat someone harshly when they leave, everyone in the company thinks, "That's how I'll be treated when I leave because that's how we treat people."

The awkwardness of employees leaving gets played out throughout the entire world every day. Many have no training on how to do it well, so a lot of times it feels like a bad dating break-up rather than conscious uncoupling—full of strong emotions, both good and bad. Some companies feel betrayed, others act like you've abandoned them. Not to mention the many exits that happen under the cloud of discord. But, it doesn't have to be this way.

I would like to boldly propose that every single company adopt this last core value:

Allow people to leave with dignity.

Allowing people to leave with dignity and respect is one of the greatest parting gifts you can give them. It's better than a going away party or a gold watch. And there is a right way and a wrong way to do it. And before I tell you the stories of how I came across this core value, let me share another insight with you.

Every person wants to hear these three simple things when they leave:

1. We're sorry you're leaving.
2. Your contribution mattered.
3. Thank you for the time you gave us.

It's that simple, and while it can be hard in practice, I promise you the effort is worth it. How you treat an employee when they leave the company can have one of two results: You will create an army of cheerleaders who tell everyone what an amazing company they worked for, or an army of shit talkers who can't wait to tell everyone how petty and classless you are.

It is my great hope that I give you this tool so that you create more cheerleaders than haters.

THE FORESHADOW

The day I decided to leave Rackspace, I was a director of project management working on amazing projects to help the company automate and scale its old systems and processes.

About a year earlier, I had met with Graham to vent

about certain parts of the organization. His words were a premonition:

> *"Lorenzo, based on your strengths, there are two main reasons you will leave Rackspace. The first one is when you don't believe in the mission of the company anymore. When the mission doesn't align with your belief system, you will leave. The second reason is simpler. You are a person who has to be able to affect change. And when you can no longer affect change, you will leave Rackspace."*

As director of project management, my very job was to introduce change. I could not have been in a better position to stay at the company, but since the IPO, implementing change had become more difficult. While I wanted to keep pushing new change that I knew would help our customers and Rackers, there were some people who fought any and all efforts with everything they had.

The last straw was an automation tool we were working on for billing and contract processing. We had developed a way to automate a process that currently took about seventeen thousand entries of manual data entry every single week.

I thought this was a great project that would change employees' lives. If I was the person having to manually enter mind-numbing data entry, I would be praying for someone to come along and put my skills to better use. My fellow project manager, Jake Gracia, was wiser than me and told me that before we pitched it, we needed to get assurance that the company wouldn't fire all the data entry people. It was a brilliant suggestion, so we took it to the very top of the company. We met with our CEO Lanham with what seemed to be a straightforward request. We told him we had found a way to save an inordinate amount of time, and more importantly, the automation would remove human error and save the company pain.

Lanham quickly saw its value, but also he agreed with Jake. He wrote us an email stating in writing that if all that automation went away, he guaranteed that no one would be fired, and we would find other roles in the company for them.

Jake and I went to the billing department, gave them our pitch, and got crickets. I could tell in the meeting that they absolutely did not want the change, but they didn't have a good reason why. They created an elaborate game of volleying the decision back and forth to my boss. For months we tried to get this pushed through, but it was obvious that someone was protecting their turf. I was so angry that I started venting to people I knew about the situation, which I (obviously) shouldn't have done.

One day, my boss, a wise, kind man named Michael Hardwick, pulled me aside and said, "Lorenzo, I just received a complaint about you from the billing department. They said you are going around telling everyone that they are a bunch of cock walkers."

I looked at him and said, "Michael, those guys are so incompetent that they can't even get my insults correct. I am calling them cock *blockers*, not cock *walkers*. And yes, I am calling them that because that is what they are."

He was a good guy, and all he did was give me a talking to. But that is when I realized that my ability to affect change at the company was over. The realization that the change I wanted to make was the right thing for the company and that it wasn't going to happen confirmed Graham's prediction; Rackspace was now a place that did not match my level of change. When I combined that with the fact that I was uninspired by the new mission of making money for shareholders, I knew it was time for me to leave.

A STARTUP CALLED CITYVOICE

Once I told myself I was leaving the company, things really went fast. The first thing I did was schedule a meeting with Rackspace's oracle of HR, the great Karla Fulton, aka Mama Karla.

Mama Karla had been at the company so long that I remember her walking from floor to floor, personally handing everyone their paychecks. She was wise, fair, and always gave me great counsel when I needed it. I told her that I had decided to leave and like a good mother, she let me vent and told me to keep her in the loop as I moved forward with my plan.

My best friend Dax had left a couple of months earlier, causing a big commotion. He left to go to one of our biggest competitors at the time, a Canadian hosting company called Peer1 Hosting, which conveniently had an office in San Antonio. Naturally, I called Dax and asked if they were hiring. He wasted no time and got me lined up with two interviews and I was in motion.

I had another really close friend who called me when he heard I was looking. My friend Matt Schatz had been one of Glenn Reinus' right-hand men. Matt was the very first sales manager to manage the BDC team when it was created. He and I were also roommates when I moved to London and he became like a brother to me. My respect for him was as high as that I held for Graham himself. Matt called and told me that he was now CEO at a small startup called CityVoice that did SEO marketing. He told me to just come by and see the office.

When I went to visit it, the startup look-and-feel hit me like a ton of bricks. It was small and scrappy with what looked to be second-hand cubicles. If that wasn't appealing enough, I found out that one of the three founders of Rackspace, Pat

Condon, had invested in the company. David Bryce had joined, and Glenn Reinus was thinking about joining the board. Those three details were too much for me to overlook. I didn't know anything about SEO, but I did know one thing, Matt Schatz, Pat Condon, David Bryce, and The Don were a winning team if I ever saw one. So, I called Dax and told him I was going to go the startup route. He did what a good best friend does and supported me 100 percent.

Next, I went to Mama Karla and told her that I was going to join CityVoice. She, too, was happy for me.

The day I planned to resign was a Monday. I had spoken to Pat Condon to strategize about how I would exit in the most respectful way. There had been a recent trend of old-school Rackers starting to leave, and it was freaking out a lot of people. Pat Condon told me that he was going to personally call the executive team and tell them that I was not going to a competitor but rather to a company that he was involved in. After he made that call, he would text me that the coast was clear for me to turn in my notice to my boss Michael. The plan was set. I told Karla Fulton I was planning on putting in my two weeks.

HERO TO ZERO

That Monday, I walked into the office, logged in, and waited. Pat Condon texted me a couple of hours later and said that he couldn't get ahold of them. There was a company leadership meeting offsite that week, and all the senior leaders were there. He said he left a voicemail, but I could go ahead and turn in my letter of resignation.

I turned it in to my boss Michael Hardwick. He was sad but gracious and told me everything I wanted to hear. I felt like a weight had been lifted, and I went back to my desk to start my two-week process of winding down my workload.

A couple of hours later, Michael came to my desk and asked to speak to me in a conference room. His flustered, stressed face told me something was bothering him. He told me that somehow the message of me leaving had gotten mixed up at the top. He asked me again if I was going to CityVoice and not a competitor. I showed him all my texts and even my CityVoice offer letter. He then told me that he didn't know how it had happened, but something had gone wrong. Our CEO had apparently got confused and thought I was going to Peer1 Hosting. He then had called the Rackspace security team and told them to have security escort me out of the building.

The only reason it didn't happen was because Mama Karla intercepted the message and started a fight with them so they couldn't walk me out. She had to pull our COO Mark Roenigk out of a meeting to get the order stopped.

I could tell that Michael was conflicted about whether or

not he should have told me, but I am glad he did. I think it hurt him, too, to see how they were going to treat me.

> ## BUSINESS LESSON: DON'T TREAT EMPLOYEES LIKE CRIMINALS
>
> Companies worry about employees going to work for a competitor and giving away the secret sauce or handing over all their customers. As soon as they learn an employee is leaving to go to a competitor, they call security, who hovers over the employee while they pack a box with their personal belongings and then escorts them to the front door. No hugging former coworkers, no tipping the barista in the lobby, just go directly to the parking lot. The only lasting sign they ever worked there will be the guard's boot print on their butt.
>
> This draconian practice operates out of anger and hurtfulness. Treat your future ex-employee with dignity and respect. Give them the opportunity to say their goodbyes, then send them home with two weeks' pay.
>
> If they were planning on stealing your secret sauce or all your customers, they've already done it anyway.

My heart broke that day. I didn't want anyone to see me cry at work, so I waited until I got home. I didn't cry out of sadness. I wept out of betrayal and anger. I had started at Rackspace when I was twenty years old. I was thirty when I resigned. I gave Rackspace my twenties. I had trained countless people and served our customers well. And in one instant, none of that mattered. In one instant, they were ready to have security unceremoniously walk me out of the building. What made it hurt so much was that it had come from the CEO. We all carry wounds from painful parts of our career, but I will tell you straight up, that was one of the biggest wounds of my career.

My last two weeks were so hard after that. I couldn't concentrate because all I could think about was how betrayed I felt. During those two weeks, there was an open book that would be the last one I ever attended. I went to it and our CEO was standing at the door as Rackers entered. I walked up to him and put my hand out to shake hands. He just looked at me in anger, shook my hand and held it as he shook his head at me repeatedly. It was as if he was saying, "I can't believe you are leaving, you traitor. How dare you."

I could not believe I was being treated this way. I went back to my desk and I just stared at my computer screen for what seemed like ten hours. Then I thought to myself, *"Screw this. I'm not going out like this. If they won't treat me with class, then I will show them that I won't stoop to their level."* I then did what I do best. I wrote a farewell email where I thanked the leaders of the company for giving me the opportunity of a lifetime. The letter is below.

Hello Everyone,

For those who don't know me, please forgive the spam. For those that do, I just wanted to send my final farewell as a

Rackspace employee. After 9 glorious years, it is finally time for me to begin a new chapter in my life. This Friday will be my last day, but before I leave, I wanted to send some long overdue "thank yous" out.

- Thank you, Rackspace for hiring a kid that was 20 years old, no college degree, never been on a plane, and never left the state of Texas. You, without a doubt, changed my life forever.
- Thank you, Rackspace for loving me until my 30th birthday, sending me to UT for a mini MBA course for free, putting me on my first plane to London, and endangering the lives of dozens of Rackers by having them report to me. I hope I didn't ruin too many lives.
- Thank you, Rackspace EMEA for showing me that traveling is the greatest education someone can ever get, that the sun is completely overrated, that loud Americans are in fact the root of all evil, and that an English breakfast is the only way to cure a hangover.
- Thank you, Mama Shannon and Mama Karla, for being who you are. The women behind the scenes of this great company, hugging those that need encouragement, crying with us in our tragedies and triumphs, and loving us into greatness.
- Thank you Graham, Lanham, and Lew. You changed the way I look at the world, the way I look at business, and the way I look at myself. I truly believe that you three have no idea how much you shaped the lives of so many

Rackers, and, as a result, generations to come. You have also altered the destiny of this community and for that I stand in complete awe of you.

- Thank you to the great friends and mentors of my life, Shannon Forester, Jake Gracia, Khaled Saffouri (The LBP: Lebanese Brad Pitt), Darren Norfolk, Brian Thomson, and Pravesh Mistry. As the great quote goes, "As iron sharpens iron, so one man sharpens another."
- Thank you to the original Team A crew, The Tequila Thursday crew, The P2 crew, and WinA for showing churn what a real ass-kicking looks like; that the underdogs always prevail; and that you can come in on a Friday and function on only 20 percent of your motor skills.

If you aren't too busy this Friday evening, please feel free to come by Pacific Moon on 281 and Brook Hollow for some going away drinks.

Boom.

I wrote this email and sent it out to the Rackspace global email list and in one click, it hit every single Racker in the company all over the world. I got farewell emails from Rackers all over the world and it made me smile. I printed every single one of them out and took them home with me.

After my farewell email, they changed the rules so that only executives could send emails to the entire company.

My exit of Rackspace could not have been a more painful one, but in the end, I decided that I would leave with my head held high and take the high road, even if they didn't. I wanted them to tell me thank you, but they didn't. So, I thanked them instead, and I walked out the door.

THE CURSE OF THE EXIT

After I left Rackspace, I noticed that what had happened to me turned out to be pretty commonplace. The company had developed a bad habit of loving someone, until they didn't. And then in what seemed like an instant, everyone turned on you, and you were out—it was like *Mean Girls*, the public company version. Wear the wrong outfit, and you are out, just like high school. I saw so many leaders turn off people when they left and treat them like outcasts just because they were leaving only to have it happen to them when their time came. So many great Rackers were unceremoniously pushed out and it had nothing to do with going public or the new breed of hires. It happened because no one had ever expected to see the mass exodus of good people. And because we thought it would never happen, we had this huge gaping hole where this core value should have been. And because it was not there, we had allowed this rotten behavior to take root in our culture.

I saw this happen with my close friend Khaled Saffouri. We had started on the same day but Khaled's ascent into sales leadership was astronomical. He was beloved by the sales team and never took a day off in ten years. But like so many old-school Rackers, he ruffled the feathers with one of the new executives. Before long, he had it out for Khaled.

I don't know what exactly happened that gave this guy the opportunity he wanted to push Khaled out. I do know it had nothing to do with Khaled's performance because he was a quota-hitting machine. Whatever it was, this new executive and HR were coming for Khaled and he knew it.

He called me one day and said, "I decided I'm going to quit tomorrow on my terms before they fire me." And he did. It was not the way a fourteen-year Racker like Khaled should have left. He was a legend in all the best ways.

Graham was moved by his leaving and sent the entire company a nice farewell email. But that wasn't enough. Khaled felt exactly as I did. He had wanted to hear the three things that all employees want to hear. But instead, Rackspace sent him out into the world as if he were a traitor.

THE JOB OFFER

Khaled called me shortly after he left and asked me to meet him at the bench of our local coffee shop. He told me that a huge-ass tech company, that we will refer to as H.A.T.C., had reached out to him and wanted to recruit him to move to Dallas and run their cloud division.

On any normal day, this would have been out of the question. Rackspace had given Khaled and I so many amazing experiences and memories. And Khaled had invested very wisely in Rackspace stock and made out very well. But Rackspace had hurt him when they pushed him out. So when H.A.T.C. called, something that would have been unthinkable was now an option because of the emotion of betrayal. Khaled took the call, and the recruiter could smell blood in the water.

Their offer came in fast and hard. It started at $400k, then went up to $500k. The final offer was close to $650k, with another $150k in bonuses for a grand total compensation of $800k.

We met at the bench again and he showed me the offer. He didn't have to say anything to me because I knew what he was thinking. He and I both loved Rackspace, but they had violated the last core value and wounded us both. I could see his wheels turning. This would be his chance to settle the score.

If he took the job, the damage he could inflict on Rackspace would have been spectacular. First off, he knew how to sell against Rackspace because he knew them so well. Second,

Khaled was beloved by his sales organization. He was like those Roman generals that weren't allowed to cross the Rubicon River into Rome because they were too powerful and could take over the city.

Khaled could call only one of his former reps, and it was all over. If he recruited one sales rep, there would have been a hundred sales reps ready to leave and go work for Khaled at H.A.T.C., no exaggeration. All this because one bad executive did not let him leave with dignity. And because of that, Khaled perceived Rackspace as the enemy.

I was very conflicted at the time because Khaled is like a brother to me, but so was Graham. Khaled went home to sleep on it and that night, I couldn't shake my angst. I decided to make a call. I called Graham and said, "You guys have a big problem on your hands. H.A.T.C. just offered Khaled $800k to go work for their cloud division and he is seriously considering taking it."

Graham was stunned. He said, "That doesn't make any sense, H.A.T.C. is like the military, Khaled would hate it there. There are so many logical reasons why it's a bad idea."

I told him, "That is your problem right there, Graham, you are thinking about this logically. Khaled is hurt and wounded, and this decision is coming from that place of hurt, not logic. All he wanted to hear when he left was that you were sorry that he left, that his contribution mattered, and you appreciate the time he gave the Rack. That is all he wants to hear."

"Leave it with me, I will get it taken care of." Graham said.

The next day Graham went into the office of Taylor Rhodes, the CEO of Rackspace at that time. Graham said to him, "Don't ask me why, but a wise man would say you need to make up with Khaled."

Taylor responded with, "It's so funny you should say that. I've been thinking about him a lot and he's been on my heart. I will do that right now."

That same day I got a call from Khaled. He asked me to meet him at the bench. I sat down and he told me that Taylor had emailed him, and he read me the email. It was thoughtful, kind, and full of grace. And in one email, Taylor did what the entire leadership team should have done in the first place. He gave Khaled the dignity and respect he deserved. He gave him the last core value.

He said things like,

> *"Khaled, as I hope you remember hearing me say time and time again, you are one of the warriors who built Rackspace from nothing into a great culture and a great company."*

And

> *"You built the Rackspace sales machine well before I got here, and I never had more fun than when we were slaying the competitors and winning business together. You are and always will be one of our most iconic leaders, and though you don't need my invitation to be here, I hope you know you are always welcome here."*

We are sorry you left, your contribution mattered, and thank you for your time with us. We all want to know that our time at a company was not a waste. We all want to be celebrated when our contribution was special and mattered.

Taylor Rhodes gave all that back to Khaled in one email. As Khaled read the email, I could see all the anger and betrayal drain from his heart and soul. Taylor had healed the wound and given him the right kind of closer.

Khaled turned to me and said, "You know what else? Rackspace was good to both of us and really changed both of our lives. I don't think I am going to take that job at H.A.T.C."

And just like that, it was the coup d'état that was never to be. Why? Because Taylor Rhodes, when called upon, intuitively knew that the last core value is the way everyone should leave.

There are very few principles that I believe every company

should have that are the same, but this is one of my exceptions. It's so important that I would argue it is the core value that you didn't know you needed. It's that important, and how do I know that? Because I put it up against an $800k offer and it won. That's how I know.

KEY TAKEAWAYS

- Treat outgoing employees with the same respect you gave them during the days they dedicated to your company.
- Your core values, culture, and social contracts should apply to offboarding as much as they do to onboarding; write down how you'll offboard employees who choose to leave.
- When an employee leaves, make sure they know you're sorry they're leaving, their contribution mattered, and you appreciate the time they spent with you.

Conclusion

For several years the nonprofit Teach for America was able to recruit the highest percentage of Ivy League students, even more than Google. How was that possible? Why would someone defer a great salary and awesome experience at Google to go work in a troubled inner-city school for two years?

They do it because Teach for America offers an inspiring mission to the valued members of their winning team.

I first heard the Teach for America data point and phrase when Graham Weston gave a TEDx Talk at Trinity University in 2010. Ironically, it was just days before I would hand in my resignation. I was bummed that I'd just heard this paradigm-shifting phrase from Rackspace's chairman, but it also helped me resolve why I was leaving. We were a winning team as a company. I was a valued member of that team. But I'd stopped believing in the mission.

I ran through my career at Rackspace like a movie reel, reliving all the moments. In each one, I could apply the moments when I felt great—a valued member of that winning team on a mission. And when I felt less than great, one or more of those three pieces was missing.

I started thinking about successful companies, and every one of them passed the test of the equation. In that moment, I realized that it's a foundational principle that any organization could build on for years to come. Everyone in the room that day knew how powerful the statement was when they heard it.

While even good things sometimes end, I hadn't quite gotten Rackspace out of my system yet.

THE CULTURE PROJECT

I had left Rackspace and was working on developing a coworking tech space in downtown San Antonio. By this time, Lanham had left and Graham was still on the board, but there was a new CEO, Taylor Rhodes. As a former Racker, whenever big seismic shifts would happen, old-school guys like Dax and me would get lots of calls from current Rackers telling us all the drama and venting. I was working on Geekdom and The 80/20 Foundation and trying to recruit startups to set up shop in San Antonio. I had nothing to do with Rackspace. One day, my phone blows up; Dax's phone blows up. We learned there had been a budget cut and a layoff that they were trying to call anything but a layoff. They cut at least thirty project managers.

Because I'd worked for Taylor Rhodes and had a great relationship, I called him, saying I was calling as a courtesy and that I'd heard about some personnel changes. I asked, "Have you ever read the book *The Hard Thing About Hard Things*?" Yes, he'd read it, he loved it, and he read it twice. I mentioned the chapter on how to do a layoff. Author Ben Horowitz opened all of his chapters with gangster rap quotes. "Do you remember the section," I asked Taylor, "where he opens with a quote that says, 'If you are going to eat shit, don't nibble'?" Yes, he remembered it.

"Rackspace did a layoff," I said, "but whoever the leader was didn't call it a layoff and did the complete opposite of the entire chapter that Ben Horowitz wrote about. Now a bunch of A players at your company are wondering what you're hiding. 'Are we in bigger trouble? Are there more coming? Should I preemptively go work somewhere else so I can still be an A player somewhere?'"

In his book, Ben Horowitz talks about being totally transparent, not for the people who are leaving but for those who are staying. "You guys didn't do that," I told him. Taylor thanked me for the feedback and said he was on it. He called a company meeting that very day at Rackspace and said, "This is an error on our part, but we did a layoff. Let's just call it a layoff and say why we did it." He announced the plan forward for all the people who were staying, executing the Ben Horowitz playbook with precision.

Because I can't help opening my big mouth, a week later Graham called me and said Taylor wanted to hire me as a contractor to help them do some culture stuff. I was reluctant. I just wanted to give advice from afar, throw potatoes over the fence and go back to my job. But Graham thought I should do it. So, I signed up to do a yearlong culture project.

They were losing old-school Rackers at an alarming rate, and they happened to be a lot of people I knew. I started cold-calling these people, doing a good, old-fashioned taxonomy, trying to identify the common threads of why they were leaving. Some telltale signs started emerging. I went back to the valued member, winning team, inspired mission—that's what kept popping up during these interviews.

I started with around twenty to thirty people. As soon as people saw that I'd been hired, they came out of the woodwork to talk to me. When you're in pain as they were, it's easy to say, "Lorenzo owns the culture stuff." But like diversity, you can't have someone own it. Everyone must work together to address problems and course-correct what's going on and change bad behavior. I had an open-ended interview style. I would simply ask them to tell me their Rackspace story, and people started talking. I would just take notes.

One woman said that they had outsourced all of the division to contractors. How can you be passionate about your work and feel like a Racker when you aren't given the courtesy of being an actual employee? You don't have to *treat them like friends and family* because they technically aren't. They purposely kept them as contractors to keep the rates low. Everyone seemed to have their own painful story, and good people were leaving because of it.

"PEOPLE LEAVE MANAGERS, NOT COMPANIES"

I presented my findings to Rackspace's SLT, the small leadership team.

The sad thing about it was, about halfway through my research, I realized these behaviors couldn't be changed unless every member of the SLT was on board with it. When I arrived at the first meeting to present to the company leaders, many were excited to see me because I had known them. A lot of them were hoping I was the silver bullet or had found the silver bullet. In my gut I knew that if they didn't all passionately rally around this topic, they were literally paying me for nothing. I felt a lot of dysfunction when I walked in there, a lot of turf wars. The findings I was there to present were not going to be popular. I was going to talk about middle management syndrome, fairness, politics, and all these taboo subjects. I was telling them that their culture had stage five cancer while an existential threat was beating them to the ground, a threat called Amazon Web Services. I essentially told them, "Know I'm giving you the gold here, but I know that you are not incentivized to rally around this. This is chemo."

No one's going to willingly opt for chemo when you've also got Amazon taking punches at you every day. I did my best, knowing if I didn't have 100 percent buy-in at that meeting, at that level, nothing was going to change. One guy on the SLT, when we got to the slide that quoted Marcus Buckingham's famous saying, "People leave managers, not companies," got very defensive. "There are many reasons people leave," he said. "That's not the main one."

I thought to myself, *You don't know this, Mr. VP, but your head of HR has shown me the exit interview data. It's literally the number one category people leave for.* What would it behoove me to say it? This was not the hill I was going to die on. I sat there in silence. I would not be able to convince him the company had cancer. That wasn't my job. I didn't have a vested interest; I didn't work there anymore. I was only a concerned third-party who was asked to help. If all

I got were blank stares, I wasn't going to press it. I said I would do my best to meet with people and encourage them. I stayed around for a couple more months and then went back to my day job.

THE CULTURE YOU MAKE

When David Bryce came up with the idea of *fanatical support*, he immediately thought of a straitjacket. He said, "I knew we needed to do something to celebrate when someone demonstrated this value." He called every medical supply company in San Antonio, and everyone hung up on him when he told them he wanted a straitjacket so he could put it on his rock star employees. Our cochairman, Morris Miller, eventually found one, and the tradition of giving out the Fanatical Straitjacket would become the highest honor in the company. David stood up and read something about the Racker and told us what they had done for our customers. They went above and beyond; they stayed up all night, all weekend. Then he told us what the customer said about this person. Maybe the person saved the customer thousands of dollars and preserved their company. Because of that, he announced he was honored to give this Racker the fanatical straitjacket. The Racker would go up and a couple other Rackers would put him in the straitjacket with Customer Service Fanatic embroidered on the back. David Bryce, the executives, and the founders would gather around to take a picture with the person. We didn't do anything the normal, cheesy way. ***Fanatical support*** was punk rock. Everyone wanted to be on that stage. Their families would come to the ceremony. To this day, photos of every employee who won the straitjacket hang on a wall at Rackspace.

Throughout my nine and a half years, I saw so many good people get the straitjacket award. I even remember being in a meeting when I was a leader and watching VPs and directors duke it out over who was worthy and who wasn't. And each and every time, I would secretly hope that I would win it one day. Getting the jacket was one of my highest aspirations, yet I never did. I may still be a teeny tiny bit bitter about it. And although I may whine about it the rest of my life, it just proves the point that I wanted it because *it was so meaningful of a tradition.*

It is not hyperbole to say that Rackspace changed my life. Deciding to be a company that cares about its people and culture is a dangerous and risky business. The truth is, it's easier to not care. People's feelings are always messy and complicated. This book is for anyone out there who is radical and punk rock enough to think that there is a better way to build a workplace.

A group of amazing women own my favorite local coffee shop, 5 Points Local. We often talk about business, and one of them told me that someone in her industry asked how she handles the high turnover of the restaurant world. She said, "I don't. Our turnover is low because people love what we are doing, and they are excited to work here." Those women get it. When you have an inspiring mission, it's not a job anymore.

My old boss Dom used to quote this famous line: "Find a job you love, and never work another day of your life." I love that quote but would tweak it a bit. I'd say:

> "Find a mission that inspires you, and never work a day in your life."

I dedicated nearly a decade of my life to the mission of Rackspace. I did a brief stint at a small startup that eventually failed. But that didn't matter, and the reason is, the job I found after that was another inspiring mission. And because I knew what to look for, I am eight and a half years into that mission.

I thought finding a company with an inspiring mission was a shooting star, a once-in-a-lifetime circumstance. I didn't think you could find it again, but you can. It's just hard to achieve and takes work.

I believe so strongly in this idea and my desire for you to experience what I did is so great that I want to end this book with a promise.

It's the promise that if you are an entrepreneur just starting out, know that you can use these stories and principles to start your company off on the right foot. You can care about people and make money. You don't have to choose between the two.

It's the promise that if you are a company that has lost its way and your culture is off track, just know that hope is not lost. That you can go back to the basics, remind people why the mission matters in the first place and rebuild from there.

It's a promise to anyone reading this who feels like they are the lone person in their company who cares about people. Take these stories and principles and share them with the people around you. I promise that you will create a tiny oasis within your organization that shines so bright it will attract people to it.

It's a promise that you can start wherever you are.

The Rack we built gave me so many amazing stories and lessons. They are my gift to you and my last act of *fanatical support*.

May you forever be a valued member of a winning team on an inspiring mission.

Acknowledgments

I want to thank my wife, Priscilla, and my stepson, Egil, for encouraging me through the entire process. Especially while I hid in a basement finishing the book.

Thank you, Ryan Hunter, for creating a cover that is as punk rock as I dreamed it would be.

I would like to thank Dax Moreno and Luke Owen, who originally helped me gain the confidence to join the technology world. I want to thank James Brehm for getting me the job at Rackspace and for my brother Danny Gomez who was constantly encouraging me when I was too insecure to believe in my abilities.

Thank you, Richard Yoo, Patrick Condon, and Dirk Elmendorf for founding a company that changed my life.

Thank you to the Rackspace leadership team who I would go into battle with against any company in the world. Thank you, Graham Weston, Morris Miller, Lanham Napier, Lew Moorman, and Glenn Reinus.

Thank you to the original Team A crew, UK Support, The Tequila Thursday Crew, P2, and WinA teams who served our customers with the highest levels of excellence I have ever seen.

Thank you to everyone who led me while I was at Rackspace: Anne Bowman, David Bryce, Frederick Suizo Mendler, Melissa Newell, Gary Boyd, Andrew Laing Gibbens, Sara Laing Gibbens, Shannon Forester-Smykay, Katie Nelson, Odus Boogie Wittenburg, Taylor Rhodes, John Lionato, Mark Roenigk, Michael Hardwick.

Thank you, Matt Schatz, Alexander Harris, Ben Frewin, Khaled Saffouri, Brian Thomson, Jon Andersson, Darren Norfolk, Ajay Rayasam, Imran Wadha, Emma Boehm, Rachel Woodson, Greg and Annette Chadbourne, Duncan Murray, Michael Johnson for taking such amazing care of me while I was in the UK.

Thank you to the UK leadership team: Dominic Monkhouse, Darren Norfolk, Jacques Greyling, Fabio Torlini, Andrew Laing Gibbens, Gary Boyd, Sarah Laing Gibbens, and Terry Connor. You gave me a once in a lifetime experience, and although some of it was a dark time for me, I will never forget that both the highs and lows made me the man I am today and for that, I am eternally grateful.

Thank you, Darren Norfolk, for all of your mentorship. Not working under your leadership is one of the greatest regrets of my entire career.

I want to thank everyone who read the book and gave me feedback during the process: Dax Moreno, David Bryce, Khaled Saffouri, Vladimir Mata, Pravesh Mistry, Charles Woodin, Priscilla Gomez, Randy Smith, David Heard, Shannon Forester-Smykay, Kathy Kersten, Kathrine Slagle, Alexandra Frey, Ryan Hunter. Special thanks to David, Shannon, Vlad, Kathy, and Katt, who sent me extensive notes and really helped shape this manuscript. It is way more accurate and flows better because of your suggestions. Thank you so much.

Thank you to the Scribe team for helping me bring this book into the world. Specifically, thank you to Barbara Boyd. You knew that what I presented at first wasn't enough for a book, but through your constant coaching and encouragement, we found the right path. It has been a great honor to have worked on three books together, and I hope to work on many more with you. Thank you also to Kayla Sokol and Mark Chait for your help editing, planning, and collaborating on this book. Thank you to JT, Zach, and Tucker. All these years later, I am still getting so much benefit and ful-fillment from what you started.

Thank you to all my friends and personal board members who are constantly there to guide me, give me counsel, and feedback: Dax Moreno, Luke Owen, Emily Bowe, Randy Smith, Khaled Saffouri, Pravesh Mistry, Bill Schley, Jake and DJ Gracia, Steve and Marisa Cunningham. Thank you to my City Church small group and the prayers you have said for me and this book. Thank you, Doug, Jess, Tim, Cody, Aly, Brett, Stormie, Lauren, Anne, Javier, Thomas, and Onnalea.

Thank you to my family for their unbelievable support and encouragement. Mom, Pops, Danny, Tara, Denise, Marco, Martha, Hector, Sonia, Jeff, Mari, Roland, and Patty. Thank you to my nieces and nephews, Andrea, Richard, Devina, Brandon, Markie, Joshua, Noah, Elisha, David, and Olivia.

About the Author

LORENZO GOMEZ III is an expert in ecosystem development, a CEO, a public speaker, and author. He has successfully helped convert a dormant urban sector of San Antonio into a thriving entrepreneurial hub. Over the last ten years, he has effectively engaged others in his vision and orchestrated their skills and strengths to create a new contemporary community of technology companies.

Under Gomez's direction, Geekdom became the #2 coworking space in Texas (2016), the #3 coworking space in the US (2015), and one of the top 25 coworking sites in the world (2016). Geekdom has grown from its humble beginnings as a small coworking space to its current membership of over 1,800 entrepreneurs, businesses, and freelancers from around San Antonio.

This is a picture from my first day at Rackspace, August 06, 2001.

In 2011, Mr. Gomez was tapped by Graham Weston, co-founder of Rackspace, to be executive director of The 80/20 Foundation, a philanthropic organization that works with and funds new and emerging nonprofits whose focus is on building the San Antonio technology ecosystem. In the last seven years, The 80/20 Foundation has given grants to nonprofit programs such as Venture for America, Students Plus Startups, and The Open Cloud Institute.

As the current chairman of the board for both Geekdom and The 80/20 Foundation, Mr. Gomez has had a positive impact on the tech industry in San Antonio, the city's economic growth and revitalization of the area. Within the five-year development period, Geekdom, at the heart of the downtown tech district, has experienced a 1,000-percent membership growth, and those members have generated 658 new jobs and $70 million in capital.

Mr. Gomez, a compelling storyteller, is the author of *The Cilantro Diaries: Business Lessons from the Most Unlikely Places*, the story of how he went from the stockroom of a grocery store to the boardrooms of two private companies, without a college degree. In his inspiring and humorous style, readers have found a story of hope and accomplishment, dedication and success. In the first week of publication, *The Cilantro Diaries* was ranked #1 in four separate categories on Amazon, including Vocational Guidance, Careers, Schools & Teaching, Career Development. The audiobook was the #1 New Release the week it debuted on audible.com, and it continues to be a top pick in the business categories, for both print and audio.

In his second book, *Tafolla Toro: Three Years of Fear*, he reaches back in time to share stories of his turbulent, traumatic, and often violent middle school years in one of San Antonio's most crime-ridden neighborhoods. He opens up to reveal the fear, anxiety, and hopelessness he felt as a teenager and how those forces shaped his life until he began taking steps as an adult to improve his mental health.

Geekdom Media is Lorenzo's newest startup venture. He co-founded Geekdom Media with serial entrepreneur, Graham Weston, with the mission to bring original content to the San Antonio ecosystem. Inspired by the impact and success of his first book, Lorenzo is now tapping other San Antonio thought-leaders to bring their skills and experience to the masses. Geekdom Media will be helping them produce high-quality, relevant books and podcasts to introduce these thought-leaders to a broader audience.

Made in the USA
Middletown, DE
11 August 2021